COP STORIES II

Policing Baltimore

A Real Conversation

Dick Ellwood

PREFACE

Since my first book, *Cop Stories-The Few, The Proud, The Ugly* was published, I have been asked by many of my fellow retired cops, and some still in law enforcement, *why didn't you tell the story about.........?*

Readers of my first book who were not in law enforcement, always ask a similar question... *are there more crazy and funny stories like you wrote about in the first book?*

Many of the stories in my first book have been labeled crazy, funny, and in some cases, unbelievable. In my writing, I have always made every effort to get across to my readers that police officers are just like everyone else. They get up in the morning, go to work like most people, interact with their peers, and get the job done. The only difference between a police officers' day at work and most other jobs is that police officers don't know if they're going home after their shift. So, I hope I portray in this book why I think police officers need to have fun on the job.

My intentions with my first book and with this book is to simply write about situations that occur every day in law enforcement...some are funny, some are serious, some are stupid, but the most important thing is that I want to paint a picture of what cops go through on a daily basis.

My hope is that after you read these cop stories, you will appreciate police officers as the human beings they are. With all that's going on in the world we live in today, we need to read about things that make you laugh and hopefully think more appreciative of the job police officers do.

Cops are just a group of men and women who take an oath to protect you from all the evil we face in our society.

Acknowledgments

I hope you enjoy these true stories in *Cop Stories II - Policing Baltimore – A Real Conversation*

My intentions are to always write about real police officers and real-life experiences within the law enforcement community. Some of the police officers that I write about in my stories are no longer with us but will never be forgotten.

I want to dedicate this book to all the outstanding men and women that I have served with during my twenty-five years on the Baltimore City Police Department. I would also dedicate the book to all law enforcement officers serving around the country.

A special posthumously thanks to some very special cops that I worked with over the years and had a tremendous impact on me. They would include; Rod Brandner, Frank Perkowski, Vernon Wilhelm, Jerry Johnson, Augie Buchheit, Jim Cadden, Furrie Cousins, and the best cop there ever was, my dad, Dick Ellwood Sr.

It is very comforting for me to know that one day, I'll be with my *guys in blue* in a place that has no crime. I'm sure we will sit around and tell some great stories.

I want to thank my son, David Ellwood, for continuing the honorable tradition of Ellwoods in law enforcement. I also want to congratulate him on his promotion to lieutenant which I learned about as I was writing this book.

So, let's get started. My guys that I have mentioned above, although no longer with us will be guiding me as I take you along for some great cop stories.

The Journey Begins...

I was not going to write another book, but as you're finding out now, I got the bug again.

This book is my fifth book and most likely will be my last. What goes into writing a book is only known by those who have done it or tried to do it. It ain't easy. The books I have written have taken me at least two years for each one of them...from start to publish. I enjoy writing, especially the true police stories that I write about. It's like going back in time and reliving some great moments and some not so great moments in my law enforcement career.

This book will be a follow-up to my first book...*Cop Stories-The Few, The Proud, The Ugly*. Of all my books, I have to say that my first book was the most exciting. I'm sure you will all agree that when you do something for the first time, it's very exciting: the first time you rode a bike, the first time you went to school, the first time you went to a ballgame, the first time you drove a car, the first time you went to Ocean City, the first time you kissed a girl or guy, the first time you got a paycheck and of course...the first time you experienced sex, especially with someone else.

As I prepared to write this new book, I wanted to reflect on the times in my life and career that I have not written about before. My first book had thirty-eight, short, true stories, about my years in law enforcement. I thought thirty-eight stories were a lot, until I started to talk to some of the cops I worked with over the years. The guys would tell me that I forgot to tell some very funny and interesting stories that they remembered.

I hope you don't mine if I take this opportunity to tell you a little about another side of me that was not law enforcement related. It may be the last time I have the forum to do so. The information and facts I will talk about are all life experiences.

So that you will know when I'm moving on to the next bit of information in this book, I will type the word...NEXT, to indicate that I'm moving on.

I have given it some thought and want to share a few things with you that I have not written about before. I hope I don't bore you before I get into the true cop stories that will be part of *Cop Stories II – Policing Baltimore – A Real Conversation.*

Let's start with the disclosure that I was a high school dropout. Not proud of it, but it happened. I went to the tenth grade at Patterson High School and simply got bored. Before Patterson, I attended Calvert Hall High School for one year. I remember that the tuition for this Catholic school was three hundred and fifty dollars. I failed two subjects and was told that I could go to summer school and make up the grades and pass to the second year.

My father was a police officer at that time and was probably making about three thousand dollars a year. When he found out about the two failing grades, he stepped in and gave me some fatherly love...*it will be a cold day in hell when I put up another three hundred and fifty dollars for you to fail again.*

Aren't fathers just great when you need them the most?

I did have the opportunity to finish high school in the Marine Corps through the Armed Forces Institute. I now have an associates degree in criminal justice and damn proud of it, even if it took seventeen years to get it. You heard me right...it took me seventeen years to get the degree. I can best explain the seventeen years this way...I was attending school on the G.I. Bill. I was also having the courses paid for by LEAP (Law Enforcement Assistance Program) through the police department. I stretched it out because I was getting monthly checks under the G.I Bill and LEAP was paying for the courses.

There wasn't anything wrong with what I did; lots of cops did the same thing. The Veterans Administration wanted veterans to go to school. The police department wanted cops to take criminal justice courses...I simply obliged them both.

As to not passing at Calvert Hall High School, I want to point out that it was my sisters' fault. My three "older" sisters were all straight "A" students throughout their school years. I had asked for their help to complete an essay for Mr. Franco, my English teacher.

It was toward the end of the year and Mr. Franco told me that if the essay was good, he would give me a passing grade. I got a "D" and my sisters need to take full responsibility for me not passing. I know when they read this, they will say it's bullshit...but it's my story and I'm sticking to it.

I'm actually not mad at them. I look back on failing that grade and wonder if it was not a blessing in disguise. Maybe if they had helped me and I passed that English class, I might have stayed in that school. I might have finished high school and gone on to college. I might have continued my education and gone to law school. I might have opened a prestigious law firm and made a ton of money. I could have been a judge. I might have gone on to be the Attorney General....... *stop this bullshit dreaming.......... ain't no way in hell my Dad was coming up with another three hundred and fifty dollars for my sophomore year.*

So, after all these years holding my sisters responsible for me quitting school, I guess I will now forgive them. If I had passed that English class, I would have also missed out on all the exciting stuff that has happened in my life over the years. I would not have the material for my books.

I don't think I would have been a good lawyer. If I had been a lawyer, my books would have had to be fiction. Lawyers lead boring lives...but they do make a lot of money. Oh well, I'm happy the way things turned out.

So, sisters, you are officially off the hook.

NEXT:

I once scored a touchdown in high school football because the opponent chasing me only had one arm. He was huge and he looked mean as hell. I really wasn't that good of a football player, but when I saw this one-armed, nasty looking guy, there was no way in hell he was catching me. I was playing running back. I remember that after scoring the touchdown, I kept running and looking back to see if the one-armed guy was still chasing me.

To top that off, the next day, the newspaper had a story about our school's win. The article talked about my touchdown...but they put my brother's name in the article instead of mine. My brother, John, went to the same school.

He swears to this day that it was really him that scored the touchdown. He tells everybody that the story about the one-armed guy was made-up. Believe me, the story is true and even to this day, I can still picture that one-armed guy chasing me.

NEXT:

I had my photo in the Baltimore Afro-American newspaper in the mid '50s. That paper is an African-American newspaper and the oldest one in the nation. Me and my buddy were playing on an all-black baseball team. We were the only white kids on the team. The name of the team was *Chick Webb*.

I found out years later that Chick Webb was considered one of the best during the American jazz and swing music era. He was born in Baltimore in 1905. He suffered from tuberculosis of the spine until his death in 1939. He was considered by many as the first *King of Swing*.

In the mid '50s, my buddy and I were about twelve years old. We never thought that having our picture in an all-black paper was a big deal, but I guess it was at that time. When the paper came out, all the black guys in the neighborhood were teasing us. I have some great memories of playing for that team and being around some great guys.

I also played on a baseball team that was managed by an extraordinary lady that later became very famous. Her name was Mary Dobkin. We all called her *Aunt Mary.*

She had one leg amputated. She got around in a wheelchair and sometimes on crutches. You might wonder how she was able to manage the team. She did have a couple of men assisting her, but she called the shots.

Aunt Mary lived in a low-income section of my neighborhood called, Latrobe Homes. The name of the baseball team was *Dobkin Dynamites*. The team was later called *AJ's Doghouse.* I remember that after games, whether we won or lost, we would go to her house for sodas and snacks.

She became so famous that they made a movie for TV about her life in 1979. You talk about an inspiration...you could not help but give it your all in sports when you watched her manage and cheer us on from her wheelchair.

Aunt Mary died in 1987 at the age of eighty-four. A newspaper article stated that it is estimated that she touched over fifty thousand children in her lifetime.

NEXT:

I was in the Marine Corps and served with Charles Whitman, the "Texas Tower Sniper" who committed mass murders back in 1966. He will always be remembered as a mass murderer. I, however, remember him as a very squared-away Marine. We served together in the early '60s at Camp LeJeune, North Carolina, home of the 2nd Marine Division.

What he did for ninety-five minutes from the twenty-eighth floor of the Texas Tower on the campus of the University of Texas was terrible. After gaining entry to the building with many weapons, he ascended to the twenty-eighth floor and commenced to shoot and kill sixteen people and wound another thirty-one before he was killed by law enforcement. Adding to this tragedy, he had murdered his mother and wife earlier in the day.

I remember that in the Marines, Whitman, was an expert with the rifle and pistol. He learned in his early childhood how to shoot from his father. His father was a firearms collector and taught his three sons to be marksmen and hunters. His father was also described as an alcoholic and a real nasty guy. It has been reported that he frequently abused his sons.

I was discharged in November 1964 and Whitman was discharged in December 1964. We were close friends in the Marines. I never had any contact with him after our discharges.

In today's world where mass shootings seem to be all too common, I often think about Whitman and wonder what went wrong. Some people would say that the Marine Corps training may have triggered it; I never saw any signs of that.

If you read about Charles Whitman, you get the sense that his father, along with being an alcoholic, was extremely strict and physically abusive with his boys. He often mistreated them for minor offenses and from an early age demanded that they be proficient in hunting and shooting.

I don't know what happened after his discharge. I will remember the guy that I knew who loved the Marine Corps. He was a spit and polish guy and could have been on the recruiting poster for the Marines Corps.

NEXT:

Just a few more words about my time in the Marines. I actually joined the Marine Corps one month after I turned seventeen. I didn't know it then, but it turned out to be the best thing I have ever done.

I was a skinny, puny, pimple-faced, kid when I went to Marine Corps boot camp. I don't think anyone in my family or in the neighborhood thought that I would make it through boot camp. I had my doubts, also.

Sixteen weeks at Parris Island, South Carolina were pure hell. When I graduated from boot camp, I knew I was a different person than when I joined. I served in the Marine Corps for four years. I knew early on that it would not be a career for me. I now look back and really do treasure that time. I got my honorable discharge in November 1964 and joined the police department one month later.

Because I served in the '60s, I am always asked if I served in "Nam". The answer is no. I got out before the Vietnam War started to intensify. I do have two brothers that enlisted…one in the Army and one in the Marines. Both my brothers went to Vietnam. I am extremely proud of their service, even though they kid me about being stationed in Washington, D.C., forty miles from home for my first two years in the Marines.

Why I joined the Marines, I will never really know. When I went to boot camp, I had never fired a weapon, had never camped out, and could not swim. A major part of boot camp in the Marines is shooting and swimming. I did all right with the shooting, but the swimming is another story. The drill instructor, after throwing me in the pool several times, asked me where I was from. I told him I was from Maryland. He said, "Isn't the Chesapeake Bay in Maryland?"

I don't think he knew, but where I grew up in the inner city of Baltimore, was nowhere near the Chesapeake Bay.

On the final test for swimming, I think I had a higher power helping me. I was able to make the mark required to complete the program. I still to this day cannot swim, maybe I could save my life...I hope I don't have to find out.

To finish up about the Marine Corps...I joined the Marines to see the world...just like the poster used to say. After boot camp, I was informed that I would be stationed in Washington, D.C. I was upset when I heard that...it's not exactly seeing the world. In fact, it's about forty miles from Baltimore, my hometown.

While in Washington, I worked in the Pentagon as a Marine guard in a highly classified area that showed the position of all the ships in the Navy. One other thing about being stationed in D.C., I was recruited to be in the Marine Corps drum and bugle corps. I had some brief training with the bugle before I went in the Marines...very brief. I was fortunate to get some training from a Marine who was very proficient with the bugle. He taught me the basics and then told me to just blow out my jaws when we played and the others would pick up the slack. I have a bugle in my home and still enjoy "attempting" to play the Marine Corps Hymn.

NEXT:

In my lifetime, I have had quite a few medical issues. I was diagnosed with Lupus and TB and after much testing, I had neither. I have had twenty-one surgeries and most were the result of playing tennis for the past fifty years. Some were minor, like hernias, carpel tunnel, trigger fingers, and nose. The others were more serious. I had surgery on both shoulders, my neck, two back surgeries, both hips replaced, my elbow, and my knee.

My tennis friends refer to me as the bionic man. When I play, it usually takes about an hour for me to put on all my braces. After the more serious surgeries, I usually said I wouldn't play anymore, but I did.

I love the game so much that as soon as I recover from a surgery and the weather is good...I'm out there giving it my best. I know that I am getting up into the *Love – 40* (tennis term), phase of my life, so my tennis days may be coming to an end.

NEXT:

By now, you have probably read enough about me, so let's move along quickly.

I'm proud of what I have accomplished over the years. Did I make some mistakes? Did I pick myself up, brush myself off, and move forward? The answer to both questions, is yes.

Without further delay, we are now ready to start *Cop Stories II – Policing Baltimore – A Real Conversation.*

I'm sure that is why you brought the book in the first place. Let me just lay out a few more things that have happened over the years. I might not get the chance in the future. I promise I will get to the stories.

I have written five books since retiring.

I arrested Mickey Mantle for being drunk in public in 1966 (first book).

I investigated a murder on death row.

I got custody of my kids in 1979 (same year as the movie Kramer vs Kramer).

I can't handle the sight of blood yet worked in a homicide unit for eleven years.

I got measured for a jock strap by the pastor of my church when I was 12 years old (no abuse took place – I don't think).

I was police officer of the year in 1967 (American Legion).

I investigated the murder of two prominent doctors in the same year.

I finished in second place in the Maryland Senior Olympics for tennis in 2007.

I was a Detective Sergeant in the homicide unit in Baltimore City.

I was the regional manager for Nationwide Insurance for Maryland/Delaware/& D.C. investigating insurance fraud.

I'm an upstanding citizen and a really all-around good guy...*standing ovation not needed but appreciated if you get the urge.*

That's enough, I have to stop. At this point I want to move forward. I'm starting to like myself more than I already do.

There will be no more NEXT, I'm starting the true *Cop Stories II Policing Baltimore – A Real Conversation.*

The beginning:

There are many things that cops see that just can't be explained. In spite of all the training and support from fellow officers, there are incidents that simply can't be explained to outsiders. I'm going to consider you an insider, and I'm going to give it my best shot in this book to tell my stories as if you were there.

You will usually only see cops sharing very detailed stories with other cops. It's hard to explain to non-law enforcement people what the situation was at the time and how it got handled. It's not like what you see on television.

Most people outside *The Thin Blue Line* cannot conceive how things are handled in crime-ridden, run-down, drug-infested, neighborhoods like those that exist in Baltimore City.

Baltimore City for many years has suffered what you might call the *Whack-A-Mole Syndrome.* If you know about the *Whack-A-Mole* game, you know that cones (moles) pop up from the holes on the board and you need to hit them with a mallet as fast as you can to get a good score. If you don't hit the mole, it goes back in the hole, only to pop up again.

In my many years on the Baltimore City PD, I have seen the *Whack-A-Mole Syndrome* up front and very close. My analogy is that if you can imagine the moles being crime, then also imagine the cops hitting the crime and making it go away.

Nothing in Baltimore City has really changed since I retired. You read in the newspaper that the commissioner and the mayor have come with a new crime strategy. So, with my Whack-A-Mole theory, the commissioner and the mayor are holding the mallet and need to hit crime so it goes away. This is usually done with the announcement that the department will be putting more officers in a high crime area. So, they hit the crime for a while, declaring it has gone away...only to find it has reared its ugly head somewhere else.

So, again using the Whack-A-Mole analogy, you need to have enough people to continuously hit the crime all over the board or in this case, the city.

When I worked in the Tactical Unit in the late '70s, we patrolled the parts of the city that were experiencing some type of crime for an extended period of time. The theory was to saturate that area with a show of force and hope that particular crime would go down. I can remember on an eight-hour shift, we would move two or three times to different areas of the city. The moves would be to an area having a problem at certain times of the day. You have to remember that criminals are not dumb. They can see that the areas they are committing their crimes are now loaded with extra cops.

I would love to read in the morning paper one day that the powers in the police department and the mayor's office have decided to start the *Whack-A-Mole Unit*, the posters could show cops carrying mallets...with the slogan being...*If you come out of your hole to commit crime, you will be whacked.*

Changing the subject:

Over my twenty-five years in law enforcement, I have been at many social functions where the men congregate to one area and the women to another. This is usually standard at most gatherings. So, if you're the only cop in the men's group, it seems that they want to hear the "gory" details of perceived police work and they are disappointed if you don't come through.

I have always found it interesting that someone would say, *Dick, tell us something crazy that happened at work.*

Hell, I could make up the goriest, craziest, fictional story, and they would be tuned in like kids hearing the *Night Before Christmas* for the first time. I have never heard anyone ask a doctor to tell them about the goriest surgery they ever performed. I have never heard anyone ask a financial guy to tell them about the most bizarre financial blunder they have ever seen. I have found out over the years, that the best approach when someone demands a cop story, is to simply say, *I can't really talk about it, the statute of limitations have not passed.*

Now, on the other hand, if I were with a group of cops, I would not only tell the story, I would embellish the hell out of it. If I had their complete attention, I would throw in a few new goodies...especially if they were not involved with the actual story. The story would be true. I would just spice it up a little.

Don't get me wrong about telling stories, I enjoy sharing stories about what I did in my years on the police department, or I wouldn't be writing books about it.

If you enjoyed reading my first book...*Cop Stories-The Few, The Proud, The Ugly*, you should naturally assume that I have many more cop stories to write about. I hope I don't disappoint you.

I'm not the only cop with stories. I'm confident that if we polled the eight hundred thousand law enforcement officers in the nation, we could write enough books to fill up many libraries.

I'm thrilled to say that I have had some success with my books. I'm not James Patterson, John Grisham, David Baldacci, or any of the famous crime writers. I'm Dick Ellwood, and I'm just as proud of my writings as the big time guys are.

After people have read my books, they tell me that they really enjoyed them. Many say that they felt as if we were just having a conversation. When I began my writing, that actually was my intention...to just write as if I were around a group of people telling a story. I hope that comes out in this book, also.

With this new book, *Cop Stories II* – Policing Baltimore – A Real Conversation, I intend to do the same thing. Why change now. I'm writing the book as if we're standing around at a party shooting the breeze. There probably won't be a Cop Stories III, so I'm going to just tell some stories and see how it turns out...just having a conversation...me and you.

I look back fondly on my career in law enforcement. I enjoyed my many years on the Baltimore City PD. I can assure you that the life of a police officer, for the most part, is very rewarding. You would not think so with all the negativity you see in the media today. No law enforcement officer knows on a daily basis how much they will have to deal with when they leave their home for their shift.

There is so much more to the job than just fighting crime. A cop, after working a single shift could leave him/her feeling satisfied, rewarded, sad, disgruntled, lonely, and fulfilled...all after that one shift.

The public, for the most part, looks at police work as to serve and protect, investigate cases, community involvement, respond to calls, and handle emergencies. Just think about it, there is no other profession that is called upon to do all this with a smile, being polite, and courteous...while also being videotaped and harassed by a certain element of our society.

In today's world, there are too many people that just stand by and do nothing when a police officer needs help. Many are hoping their video gets on the eleven o'clock news. What happened to the days when a police officer was in trouble and got help from citizens? I can assure you that during my early days walking a post in East Baltimore, I was fortunate on many occasions to get help when I needed it.

When people say that the entire city of Baltimore is bad, I say that is not true. In many sections of Baltimore, you will have the criminal element that is hell-bent on committing crime. But, in some of those same sections, you have decent law-abiding people that want nothing more than to live a peaceful rewarding life for themselves and for their family.

My intentions with my first book...*Cop Stories-The Few, The Proud, The Ugly* and also with this new book, *Cop Stories II – Policing Baltimore – A Real Conversation,* is to merely write about the life of a cop who worked in a city that he loves. I'll share the good along with the bad to show you the ups and downs that can occur during twenty-five years in law enforcement. I pull no punches for the simple fact that I want to be honest and up-front with the readers...just having a conversation...me and you.

Now, as far as this book, it may very likely be the last book that I write. I have really enjoyed writing my books and meeting many new friends. Hell, many years ago, I couldn't even get a passing grade in high school on an essay...those damn sisters of mine.

I've come a long way. I've been told that my writing is a little weird, but that's okay because I'm just trying to have a conversation….me and you. I'll tell you more about my sisters later.

Now, let's move on to that first story. That's what you bought the book for, right? Here we go…remember, this is me and you having a conversation. I'll do the talking for a while and you can sit back and be the listener. If you get tired of reading, put the book down for a bit. When you're ready to start up again, I'll be here…just me and you.

Conversation #1

Back in the late '60s, there was a carry-out sub shop on North Avenue in East Baltimore called Harley's. It was owned and operated by a very interesting character named, Harley Brinsfield. He opened several other sub shops around the city. He also had a radio show called, *Music of Baltimore* which was on Sunday nights from the early '50s until the late '70s. His stores were the first and largest fast food sub shops, way before Subway.

The problem with the store on North Avenue was that it was being robbed frequently. The store was situated on North Avenue in midtown Baltimore City, just two blocks from Guilford Avenue. Back in those days, it was known to police that worked the area, that if a crime occurred on North Avenue and the bad guys ran toward Guilford Avenue, you had very little chance of catching them. That was the M.O. of the people robbing the Harley's North Avenue store.

After several robberies at the store, the captain of the Central District decided to put two plainclothes cops in the back of the store to see if they could catch the bad guys. I was working in the Central District Operations Squad at the time and my partner and I were picked for the assignment.

A lot of planning went into just how we would set up to catch somebody robbing the store. We knew that most of the robberies were occurring after ten o'clock at night. Along with our sergeant, we met with the manager of the store. The layout of the store was such that it had an elevated area in the rear that provided a clear view of the entire store. It was decided that my partner and I would be in that spot with our handguns and a shotgun.

During all of the prior robberies, the bad guy(s) showed guns. The area in the rear of the store we would be in, provided a clear line of fire if needed. The store manager also installed a device in the cash register that would allow the employee being robbed to notify us. The device consisted of a small lever that would be attached to a twenty-dollar bill in the cash register. At the time of the robbery, the employee only had to pull that bill from the register and a red light would blink where we were positioned. We rehearsed the procedure with those working the night shift. They were instructed, that after pulling the bill from the register, the employee working the cash register would drop to the floor.

If all went well, we would come over the top of our position and announce that we were the police...proudly displaying our shotgun. If necessary and if we had a clear line of fire, we may have had to take out the bad guys, if they were armed.

The plan sounded great and we were ready to go. Along with the plan from the inside, there would be two officers in an unmarked police car across the street from the shop, in case the bad guys got out the front door. If that happened, we would notify them over our walkie-talkie.

With everything in place, we went to the store around 8 P.M. and took up our position. We wanted to get there just as it was turning dark. We talked to the employees and refreshed them on the procedure.

My partner, Joe Bolesta and I, had worked together for about a year. As a side note...Joe later went through the ranks of the police department and rose to the position of deputy commissioner. I was always very proud of him when he made rank after rank in the department. He was an outstanding police officer and I enjoyed every day that we worked together. Although I was the senior man, he was very savvy about police work.

Looking back on our time working together, we had some great cases and some very interesting incidents. We later, after the Harley's incident, worked in the Central District Vice Unit. I have written about some of our times working vice in my first book...*Cop Stories-The Few, The Proud, The Ugly.*

We were in position in the rear of Harley's just relaxing and periodically looking over the partition to see if anything was happening. At about 10 P.M. one of the employees asked if we wanted a sandwich. Knowing that we might be there for a while, we got the sandwiches and two sodas. We were eating and thinking nothing was going to happen on this night. Were we ever wrong! We heard a loud scream, dropped our sandwiches, picked up the shotgun, looked over the partition, and saw nothing but an employee standing by the cash register crying and screaming. The other two employees were on the ground.

We came down from our position and saw that the cash register was open. The twenty-dollar bill was still in position. I was screaming at the lady near the cash register and then had to physically shake her.

After screaming, *"What the hell happened?"* she tried to mouth that she had been robbed. Another employee on the floor said that they had been robbed at gunpoint and the lady at the register panicked. She did not pull the bill from the register as planned. I got on the walkie-talkie and told the guys outside that the place had been held-up at gun point. They responded by asking if we took down the hold-up men. I told them what happened and they said they did not see anyone running from the store.

Well, that's about the gist of the story, except that when the sergeant and lieutenant came to the scene, it wasn't pretty. They both started hollering at Joe and I, as if we had done something wrong. After hearing the story, they calmed down a little. The issue now was, how in the hell do we tell the captain that the store was held-up while two police officers were in the store. I suggested that we tell the truth, but the sergeant and lieutenant were old-timers and they wanted to come up with something else. They felt that this was no time to be telling the truth.

Now that the employees were calming down, we talked to the lady who was at the register. She said that two black guys came in and immediately showed guns. They demanded the money and she started to cry. She said she did not pull the twenty-dollar bill from the register because she thought that we would come over the top and just start shooting. She gave them all the money in the register except the one she was supposed to give them.

I think this incident comes under the category of...*when shit goes bad – shit really goes bad, and the best of plans can go right down the toilet.*

Conversation #2

Another story that my partner and I got involved in happened in the late '60s. We were working a two-man patrol car in the vicinity of North Avenue and Charles Street. We were working the 4 P.M. to midnight shift and things were fairly quiet until about 7 P.M. We got a call from the dispatcher for an armed hold-up in progress at Evelyn's tavern in the 100 block of North Avenue. The bar was very close to the Harley's sub shop that we talked about in our previous conversation.

A hold-up in progress usually meant that the bad guy(s) were still in the location and in the process of robbing the bar. From experience, we both knew that usually by the time police cars got on the scene, the bad guys were usually gone. The main thing was to get there as quick and as safe as possible. It is somewhat of a challenge for cops when this type of call goes out. All the cars in the area want to get there first, so the race is on.

When the call came over the radio, we were about ten blocks away from the bar. My partner, Joe Bolesta, was driving that night. He had a tendency to drive extremely fast. I was the more conservative type of driver and he often kidded me about driving like an old lady. Joe, also had a little problem with seeing distances and sometimes he scared the shit out of me going to calls.

We acknowledge the call from the dispatcher and off to the races we went. We had the running lights and siren blasting away. I knew that when we were driving along North Avenue we would encounter some traffic. I told Joe to be careful and that only made him go faster. I kept my mouth shut as I held onto my seat.

We were one block from the scene when a black man ran out in front of our car. Not sure at what point Joe saw this guy, but we nailed him and he flew up in the air. I almost messed my paints when this happened, but Joe seemed calm. As if he had only hit a tree branch, he said, "Should we stop and check on him or go to the call?"

I said, "Damn man, you just probably killed some guy and you want to know if we should stop."

17

While I'm talking, he was just continuing on to the hold-up call.

I looked back at the guy we hit and miraculously he was standing. He appeared to be brushing himself off.

We got to the bar and we ran inside with guns drawn. The owner was extremely shook-up as he was telling us that the hold-up man just ran out of the bar. He said he had a gun and got all the money.

I asked for a description to put out over the police radio. The owner told me that the guy was a black man, about six-foot-tall, wearing a green windbreaker, and had a black baseball hat on. I hope your not thinking ahead of me on what the plot of this story is...but if you are, here it is...yes, we had just hit the hold-up man with our police car.

I put the description of the guy out over the police radio. I did not mention anything about running this guy down with our car. Other units had arrived at the bar and one of them took the police report from the owner. Joe and I went outside and forgive me for saying this...we laughed our asses off. In police work, you got to have some levity and how can you not laugh about what we did.

After pulling ourselves together, Joe said that the guy we hit has to be injured pretty bad. With that in mind, we decided to drive to Maryland General Hospital which was the closest hospital in the area. We were very familiar with the hospital, we often spent time there with victims of crimes or just visiting the nurses in the emergency room.

Nurses and cops have a lot in common. We work shift work, we see a lot of crime victims, and most importantly we have a sense of humor. I talked to the head nurse and asked if anyone had come in with leg injuries. She thought for a moment and said that the guy behind curtain number five has a broken leg and some cuts and bruises on his body. I asked her to describe the guy. She said he was a black man about six-foot-tall, wearing a green windbreaker and a black baseball cap. She then laid the big one on us...she said that the guy reported that he was hit by a car and the car didn't stop. At this point we started laughing again. Not even knowing what we were laughing at, the nurse laughed with us.

We went to curtain number five and the guy was laying there, obviously in pain. You could see he was messed up. I asked him what happened.

He said he was walking across the street and was hit by a car. I asked him if the car was blue and white, with emergency lights flaring, a siren blasting, and were there two police officers in the front seat. He grimaced in pain and said, "What the fuck you talking about?"

Without putting this guy through any more agony, I told him we were the culprits that ran him over. I told him we knew he had held-up the tavern on North Avenue and could be identified by the tavern owner.

I won't repeat all of what the guy said, but it went something like this, "What the fuck you talking about?" Are you the mother f-----'s that ran me over? Damn, I'm going to sue your asses...you mother f-----'s can't get away with this!"

Well, after this dude talked about our mothers for awhile, we informed him that this might be the unluckiest day of his life and that he was under arrest for armed robbery.

The guy was charged with armed robbery when he was released from the hospital. At the trial, he took the stand and denied that he held up the tavern. He also denied that his injuries were the result of us crashing into him while he was running from the scene. I remember the judge saying to him, *do you think these officers would come into court with such a made-up story, admitting that they ran over a guy fleeing from holding up a tavern?*

The jury deliberated for about thirty minutes and found him guilty. I forget what the sentence was, but can you imagine this guy in prison telling his home-boys that he held-up a tavern and while running away, he was hit by a police car.

Nobody ever said that criminals were smart.

This was one time that my partner's erratic driving actually paid off. I still to this day, laugh when I tell this story.

Conversation #3

In 1967, the Baltimore City Police Department purchased a fleet of new Chevrolets. It was perfect timing, as the cars we had in the Central District were literally falling apart. I can remember driving a police car where I could look down and see the road through a large hole in the floor. Most of the cars were in such bad shape that the city motor pool repair shop could not keep up with the repairs.

It was actually embarrassing driving around in those cars. People would look over, stare at the car, and drive away laughing. To put it simply, the fleet was way out of date. The replacement cars were a welcome relief to the men in the district.

I was working in the Central District Operations Unit at the time. The unit consisted of about ten officers, two sergeants, and a lieutenant. We were assigned to the district but we didn't handle routine calls for service. We worked in high crime areas attempting to alleviate whatever problem was occurring in that particular area. We worked most of the time in uniform. We also would work in plainclothes on certain occasions where the need existed for unmarked cars and plainclothes officers. We would saturate an area in an attempt to catch some bad guys. This was my first experience to be working in plainclothes capacity and I was excited.

We were working the 4 P.M. to midnight shift. It was a typical, very hot, summer night in Baltimore City. Because we were working in plainclothes, we would naturally be riding in unmarked police cars. We usually teamed up with a partner, but on this night the sergeant wanted us to work alone, so that we could put more cars in the targeted area.

My partner in the Operations Unit was none other than fast driving, Joe Bolesta. I have mentioned his name many times in my stories, both in this book and my first book. I always felt safe working with him. He was a big guy, but his size was not the only reason I felt safe working with him; he was a very smart cop. He had a natural instinct for police work.

I think he felt the same way about me or at least I hope he did. We just seemed to click well with each other and that's important when you work with the same guy all the time. You get to know the qualities, capabilities, and personality of each other the longer you work together.

After roll call, the sergeant told us to go to the motor pool and each one of us was to check out an unmarked vehicle.

I think we went out on the street that night with six vehicles. The other members of the unit were on leave.

Our sergeant was Pete Bailey, one of the finest men I have ever known. He was the kind of supervisor that led by example and not by threats. Instead of sergeant, I'm calling him Pete for the rest of this story. We became such close friends from the late '60s until I retired. Our friendship continued after we both retired. If you want to read some great stories about Pete and I, you need to get my first book.

We walked across the street from the Central District to where the department motor pool was located. The procedure was that you were given keys to a vehicle, you checked the vehicle, filled out a paper on the condition of the vehicle, listed the starting mileage, and turned the paper into the officer manning the desk in the motor pool.

Knowing that the department had purchased new 1967 Chevrolets, we asked for them. I think that four of us got the new vehicles. These vehicles were like driving a Cadillac, after driving the junk we were used to. I got one of the new cars and there wasn't much to check. The vehicle had never been driven by anyone since it arrived at the motor pool. I made out the form and listed that the vehicle had about seventy-five miles on the odometer. I left the motor pool and proceeded to the area we were to patrol.

It was like heaven driving a brand new unmarked police car. I could not see the street when I looked down at the floor. The cars were equipped with police radios. We also would go on patrol with what they called, purple hand walkie talkies. These handheld walkie-talkies would allow you to get out of the car and still be in communication with the dispatcher. The walkie-talkie also gave you the ability to switch to a certain frequency that allowed you to talk to the other officers in the unit without going through the dispatcher.

There was a spot where police cars would frequent to take a break out of sight of the public. Cops would meet there to eat a sandwich, drink a coffee, or just shoot the breeze. This spot was located on a slight hill that overlooked the Jones Falls Expressway. At any given time, there could be several police cars at this spot, both marked and unmarked cars. I pulled up on the spot and there were several cars already there.

I maneuvered my vehicle up a little further on the hill. We usually stood outside our cars and talked about stuff that cops talk about…arrests made the day before, what we did on our day off, what we were going to do on our next off day, and yes, we talked about women. What the hell did you expect me to say…we talked about church, volunteering at the helping-up mission, collecting toys for needy kids.

Remember, we're cops, not altar boys…although I was an altar boy once and got measured for a jock strap by the pastor of the church. I was not abused…I don't think. That story might be for another book.

While standing around the cars and talking, a call came over the police radio. We always turned the radios up when we were out of the car, so we could hear what was happening. The call that came in was for a *"Signal 13"* at Hank's bar which was on Lafayette Street and fairly close to where we were parked. A *"Signal 13"* call is given out when a police officer needs help. It's a call in the police department that is probably the most urgent call because it means a fellow officer is in trouble and needs assistance, like right away.

When this emergency call comes out, no matter what you're doing, you drop it and get to that call as fast as possible, breaking all the rules of the road. Well, the marked police cars took off first and left a trail of dust. All of us in unmarked cars jumped in our cars and took off following the marked units…well, that would be all the unmarked cars except me. I failed to mention that when I pulled into the spot, I had backed my car up a slightly hilly area. When I jumped in the car, in my excitement and after starting the car, I put it in reverse. The car bolted back and went over the hill. If I can explain where I wound up…can you picture a space craft about to take off…that's what my car looked like. The entire rear of the vehicle was over the hill and I was completely vertical. I was sitting in the seat, knowing that if I moved or tried to get out of the car, it would probably go over the hill onto the expressway. I was all by myself, as all the other cars went to the urgent call.

I sat motionless, fearing that any move on my part would spell disaster. My only option was to embarrass myself and call for help. I waited until I heard that the call for assistance was clear. The officer was fine and did not get hurt. I was now thinking; I'm the one who needs help.

I used the walkie-talkie and called for my partner to come back to the spot. I didn't want to say anything over the police radio about the predicament I was in.

My partner and a couple of other guys responded back. When they saw me in the car and the position the vehicle was, they broke out laughing. Cops are weird like this...incidents that would shake the shit out of normal people, does not phase cops.

They stood around laughing and mocking me. I was pissed, but I was in no position to give them a hard time. I could hear them talking amongst themselves trying to figure out what the hell they could do. They decided that the only option was to call a tow truck and attempt to pull the vehicle off the hill and back to solid level ground. The guys got a tow truck from a nearby gas station that we frequented and knew the owner.

When the tow truck arrived and after the driver laughed so hard, he probably pissed his pants. He told me that no matter what, do not touch the brake or make any kind of moves. He hooked a wench onto the vehicle and said he would try to slowly lower the vehicle to the ground. Well, slowly didn't really work, he did lower me and the vehicle, but it crashed to the ground really hard.

I got out of the vehicle and could only lean against the car. I was shaking, laughing, and probably crying a little bit. I could hear the guys talking about the damage to the vehicle. The only thing I was thinking about was that I was probably going to get fired for messing up this new vehicle.

With a situation this bad, I had to call Pete and tell him what happened. When he arrived, and looked at the vehicle, what he said can't be repeated in this story. We talked it over and came up with a few ideas on what we should do. We could take it to a repair shop and see if they could pull out the larger dents.

23

We could say it was parked and someone ran into the rear of the vehicle. We could simply take the vehicle back to the motor pool after my shift and see if anyone noticed the damage. Being the good decent and honest cops that we were, we decided on idea number three.

I drove the vehicle to the motor pool at about midnight. The procedure would be that the motor pool officer on duty would do a cursory check of the vehicle. He usually stood outside the office as you drove the vehicle in.

I drove the vehicle into the motor pool and he just waved me on. I parked the vehicle. I purposely backed it into a spot so that the damage could not be seen. I left the garage and went home.

The next day I got a call early in the morning from the sergeant that was the supervisor of the motor pool. This guy was hated by everyone in the department. He was just a nasty, old, fat bastard. Without even saying who he was, like I didn't know from his voice, he commenced to holler over the phone that I wrecked one of his new cars. I let him rant on and on and finally he said, "What the hell happened to the car you checked out last night?"

I figured, what the hell, we went this far, I might as well go all the way. I said in a hopefully convincing voice, "Sarge, I don't know what happened to the vehicle. It was fine when I turned it in last night."

He hollered and screamed some more…so loud that I had to hold the phone away from my ear. Without saying much more, he told me to be in his office that day prior to my shift.

I called Pete at home and told him what happened. He told me not to worry. He said that he would go with me to the nasty old sergeant's office. We showed up early and before the sergeant could say anything, Pete got to him first. Pete told him that he personally saw the vehicle before I turned it in and it did not have any damage. He told him that the vehicle was inspected by the motor pool officer when it was checked in. The nasty old sergeant started to talk, but Pete stopped him. "If the vehicle was checked by your man last night and I checked it also, you need to find out who took it out after midnight, that's the guy you need to talk to".

The fat slob sergeant didn't know what to say. Pete and I walked out of his office. The sergeant was hollering something to us as we made a quick exit.

We walked across the street to the Central District. From that encounter forward, I never heard back from that motor pool sergeant.

A funny situation like that usually gets around in the department. I worried for quite a while that the actual story would make its way back to the nasty old motor pool sergeant...but it didn't.

Conversation # 4

This conversation is unrelated to police work. It actually takes me back to my childhood. Hang with me and then we will get back to the cop stories.

I grew up in a great neighborhood in East Baltimore. In the mid to late '50s, many of the white families were leaving our neighborhood and moving to the suburbs. I'm not sure what caused this exit. To be honest, I think that some white families were not too thrilled about the black families moving into the neighborhood...*tell it like it is.*

My family was one of the last to move from our neighborhood in the early '60s. When the neighborhood was changing, it really didn't bother me. I didn't miss a beat. Me and my long-time buddies quickly made friends with the new black kids moving in that were our age.

I can honestly tell you that when you're a kid that loves sports, it doesn't matter what color your friends are...it only matters if they are available on a hot summer day to hang out and play sports.

We played baseball from early in the morning until it got dark. We played on a hard-top field at the Ambrose J. Kennedy playground. Not sure who Ambrose was, I think he was some kind of politician with the city. I do know that he was not related to the real Kennedys.

I have written about that playground in my first book. Here's where I'm going with this story. I have, like most people witnessed bouts of racism throughout my life. I'm writing about it to show some incidents that occurred from the '50s thru the '60s.

When I joined the Marines, I was seventeen. I remember being at the U.S. Custom House in downtown Baltimore City waiting for the bus to take us to the train station. The train would then take us to Parris Island, South Carolina, where boot camp for the Marine Corps was conducted.

There were three guys from Baltimore going to boot camp that day. Along with me, there were Billy Gibson and Robert Harrell. Gibson was a red-headed hillbilly type guy from Essex, Maryland. Harrell was a black guy from West Baltimore.

We got on the empty bus and each took a separate seat and didn't say anything. When the bus pulled away, Gibson looked directly at Harrell and said, "I didn't think the Marines took "Niggers" in the corps." *(I use that word to make sure you get the full effect of the situation)*

Well, when I heard that, I was sure there would be some fighting before we even joined the Marines. Harrell, seemed to always have a smile on his face. The smile would later get him in a lot of trouble in boot camp. Harrell looked back at Gibson and said, "I guess if they take skinny, red-headed, white boys...I see no reason why they would not take a nigger."

At this point, the bus driver got involved. He stopped the bus and told Gibson and Harrell that they should save their fighting words for boot camp. I'll continue here with our conversation but I want to tell you that Gibson and Harrell later became good friends during and after boot camp. It was a rocky start, but the Marine Corps has a way of making you pull together no matter where you come from or what color you are.

Marine Corps boot camp is not for the timid or weak. Back in those days, if you could not take both physical and verbal abuse from the drill instructors, you probably should not have joined the Marine Corps.

In 1960, the Marine Corps was predominantly made up of white guys. In my platoon in boot camp we had fifty-five recruits and only three were black guys. During the sixteen weeks of boot camp, the black guys caught hell from the two white drill instructors. I don't think that if I were black, I could have made it through. The senior drill instructor, Sergeant Stafford, was the meanest looking man I have ever seen. He had a southern draw when he spoke; he had to be from the Deep South. I'm sure that's where his hatred for blacks started. There were a few times in boot camp that I caught so much abuse that I thought I was black.

Boot camp was tough for me because I had never fired a weapon, I was skinny, and I had never been away from home. I certainly took my share of verbal and physical abuse by the drill instructors...but that was what the Marine Corps was about back then.

Seeing how the black guys were treated made me feel sorry for them. I'm sure I was outnumbered in the feeling sorry for the black guys. The majority of our platoon was white and from the South.

Marine Corps boot camp is a one-way street...you have no say. You only speak when your spoken to and strive to make it through. The drill instructors always told us that the only way off the island was to graduate from boot camp or run for it and try to swim with the alligators. I hate alligators and can't swim, so my way off the island was to put up with all the bullshit and make it through sixteen weeks of hell.

Harrell took all that the drill instructors could give out. If we were told to do fifty push-ups, they would tell Harrell to do a hundred. He never hesitated and because he was in such great shape, he could do them with no problem. You could never upstage a drill instructor; they are hard to the core. The training they get to be a drill instructor is very intense. Their job is to take a group of young boys and turn them into men or as the D.I. would say, *mean lean fighting machines.* I do actually believe that their mission from the day you set foot on the island, is to transform you from a civilian, to a member of the greatest fighting force in the world. Unfortunately, some don't make it and are either sent packing or crack under the pressure.

Harrell not only made it through boot camp, he was awarded for being one of the top recruits in the class. He was promoted to private first class at our graduation ceremony. Being promoted right out of boot camp is quite an accomplishment. In our recruit class, we had four Marines promoted to PFC after boot camp, three white guys and Harrell.

Harrell and I became good friends in boot camp. On several occasions he had to give me a little pep talk to get me through some crazy activity and some downright stupid shit that the drill instructors came up with. He was an inspiration to me. I saw the way the drill instructors treated him. His courage and tenacity made me want to exceed, so that the white kid from East Baltimore and the black kid from West Baltimore would be Marines.

I remember when we graduated from boot camp and we were presented with the Marine Corps emblem...the globe and anchor, it made you feel ten feet tall. Everything you went through to get to be called a Marine was now worth it.

When we were boarding the bus to take our first leave, I watched Sergeant Stafford call Harrell to the side of the bus. Sergeant Stafford was still screaming loud and using profanity. I really believe that being a D. I. was his life and that's all he knew. We assumed that he was a single guy. He lived on the base and was a heavy drinker. I guess you could say with certainty that he lived and breathed the Marine Corps.

Sergeant Stafford had Harrell near the rear of the bus, but we could all see what he was doing. He saluted Harrell and embraced him. Yes, the meanest man in the world who obviously had a dislike of blacks was embracing my man, Harrell.

He told Harrell that he was one of the finest recruits that he had ever put through boot camp. The embrace was actually one of the stiffest I had ever seen, but for Stafford it probably took all he could muster to do it.

Harrell, later told me that Stafford also told him that it would be an honor to go to battle with him. Coming from Sergeant Stafford and after all the verbal and physical abuse Harrell had endured in boot camp, I found in myself to have some respect for Sergeant Stafford...but the thought of him still gives me chills to this day.

Fast forward to when I joined the Baltimore City Police Department where I continued to see racism raise its ugly head.

I joined the police department as soon as I was discharged from the Marines. I was discharged in October and sworn in the police department in December. I started in the police academy with just nineteen guys. The makeup of our academy class was sixteen white guys and three black guys.

When we graduated from the academy in late March 1965, four of us were assigned to the Central District. It was me, Jon Grow, Paul Page, and Bernie Jackson. I was excited to go to the Central District because that is where my dad had started many years earlier. I was also excited when I was assigned to work a post in the neighborhood that I grew up in. I talked about that neighborhood in my first book, so I won't rehash that here.

The other three guys were assigned to various posts in the district. Working on my shift was Jon Grow and Bernie Jackson. Paul Page was assigned to a different shift. I will mention here that Bernie Jackson was a black guy and a really good cop. We became close friends while in the police academy. We would on occasion get together with our families at each other's home. I kind of got the feeling from some of the older cops in the district that they did not quite approve of Bernie and I being such good friends.

Even though my dad was a cop, I never heard stories from him about racism in the police department. I'm sure he saw it, but I guess he kept it to himself or it was just something you didn't talk about back then. As time went on, I could see it very clearly.

The Central District had some very nice areas to patrol. In the downtown area there were great restaurants, movie theaters, and all the nice department stores. Along Charles Street there were many high-dollar restaurants. Then there were the not so good neighborhoods in the district. It took a while but I started to notice that the black guys did not get assignments in the downtown area or any of the nicer areas.

One day at roll call, the sergeant assigned Bernie to a foot post downtown. We were leaving the roll call room and the sergeant hollered out to Bernie, "Sorry Jackson, I forgot that you can't work downtown."

When Bernie asked him why, the sergeant seemed offended that Bernie didn't know why. He got right up in Bernie's face and said, "Blacks don't work downtown; didn't anybody tell you?"

I was standing close by and that was the first time I had heard that. I later asked a senior cop about it and he said that had been the policy for as long as he had been in the district. He went on to tell me that black officers were not allowed to work in a patrol car either. I was taken aback about this and felt bad for Bernie. I watched his reaction and he didn't seem to be bothered by what had happened. I was thinking that maybe Bernie had experienced this so much that he just accepted it. I made it a point to talk to him after the shift was over.

We sat in my car. Bernie was surprised that I didn't know about black officers not being allowed to work downtown. I guess he figured that if my dad was a

30

cop in that district, I would have known. I wanted to say that I was sorry that he and others were being treated that way, but before I could, he stopped me. He went on to say that prior to joining the police department, he had experienced much of the same racist behavior in the Army. He said, "Listen man, you and I are good friends. We can talk to each other, have our families get together, drink a beer…but we are different in this police department. I can take all this bullshit because I need this job. I don't mine working the bad neighborhoods because that's where my people live. It's 1965, we're new on this job, maybe one day you and I will see all of this racist stuff change. But, until then I'll work wherever the hell they want me to work. Now, let's get out of here before that asshole sergeant ask us why we are even sitting in your car."

A few years later, Bernie quit the department. I never had a chance to talk to him before he quit. I guess he took as much as he could and decided there was something else out there that didn't have such racial tones.

As a side note, I think things did improve as the years went by. I remember in 1967 they actually assigned a black police officer to work a patrol car with a white officer. In those days, the police vehicles were painted black and white. The colors of the car were fitting, because everyone called it the black and white car and they didn't mean the paint job.

I can honestly say that as my career went on in the department, I worked with some of the finest black police officers you would ever want to know.

Later in my career I got promoted to sergeant. I made sure that every officer working for me was treated with the respect they deserve.

I never saw black or white officers…I only saw blue officers.

Conversation # 5

I have mentioned previously that I was in the Marine Corps. I was very proud of my service. When I would have the opportunity to meet other Marines, we always talked about how it was when you were in. I have met many Marines over the years and in the mid '70s when I was going through a divorce, I lived with two Marines.

I have a story to tell about an incident that does not make me proud to write about, but I'll do it anyway. It's not about anything I did wrong; it's about an arrest I wish I didn't have to make.

I was working on Charles Street. I have already told you that Charles Street back in the '60s and '70s was an area that had the finest restaurants and bars in the city. On any given night, you might run into the governor, mayor, sports figures, TV personalities, and pretty much the elite of Baltimore. I was working the midnight to 8 A.M. shift and it was extremely cold. It was so cold that I remember wearing long underwear.

On that shift after the restaurants and bars closed, you had no place to get warm, thus the long underwear. I was walking north on Charles Street near Eager Street and it was about 3 A.M. There wasn't anyone walking on the street, as I told you, it was bitter cold. As I was walking, I noticed a lady walking about a city block ahead of me. I found this to be very unusual at this time in the morning. The area she was walking was fairly safe, but I wanted to make sure she got where she was going.

I walked fast to catch up with her and as I did, I noticed that she started walking faster. At first, I thought maybe she didn't know I was a police officer, but as I got closer, I saw her turn a little and I was sure she knew I was a cop. I didn't want to run up on her, but I was now concerned why she wouldn't stop. As I got even closer, I noticed that she was not really dressed for the weather. She had on a very short dress, high heel shoes, a fur wrap around her neck and she was carrying a pocketbook. As I got even closer, I could see that she had long blonde hair and appeared to be having some problem walking in the high heel shoes. I was only about ten feet behind her and was perplexed that she would not turn around and acknowledge me.

I hollered out to her, "Excuse me miss, are you all right?"

I said it loud enough that it kind of echoed off the buildings. I knew she had to hear me as it was just she and I on the street; we were very close to each other.

Even though this was a woman, I still became concerned for my safety because of the way she was acting. At no time did she turn to look at me, she actually started a little shuffling motion to go faster, but I think the high heel shoes were holding her back. I knew at this point something was wrong. I walked a couple of feet behind her and said, "Miss, I would like for you to stop and talk to me."

She stopped and moved over against a building, still not facing me. At this point, I didn't care if it was a female or not, I moved my gun from my holster to the large pocket in my coat. At that time, we were still wearing those ungodly, long, blue overcoats that unless you had your gun in the pocket, you would have a hell of a time getting it out in a hurry.

With no one around except me and her, I got into my protect-your-ass mode. This was getting stranger with every move she made. Finally, with her facing the building, I said, "Miss, I'm a city police officer. I'm not here to harass you. I'm concerned for your safety."

She said nothing and still would not face me. I even asked her if she could hear me and she nodded that she could. I began asking things like...do you live in the area, are you meeting someone, do you have a car close by, are you lost, and still got no response. I started to notice things like...her makeup appeared to be too much, her clothes were really tight, her hair looked fake...and it finally hit me...this is a female impersonator.

I got right up close to her and told her to look at me. I told her if she didn't answer me and show me some identification, I might have to detain her.

At this point, she turned to me and with the deepest voice that filled the cold dark night, she said, "I'm not lost; I know where I am. If you just allow me to catch a cab, I'll go home."

Well, I can't say that I was shocked, because I was already working on the theory that this was not a female. I told her (him) that impersonating a female was a crime in Baltimore City... (not sure if that is still the case) and I was placing him under arrest. When we got down to the station, we booked the guy and within an hour, he made a call and got out on bail.

In those days, the arrests that were made on the midnight shift were tried at 9 A.M. that morning. At the hearing the arrestee could request a postponement, ask for a jury trial, or go ahead with the sitting judge to try the case.

I was sitting in the courtroom when I saw a Marine staff sergeant in full uniform enter the courtroom. As a Marine myself, I took notice that he seemed very squared away in his uniform including several medals pinned on his chest.

The court clerk called out a name and this Marine walked forward to the trial table in front of the judge. He had two people dressed in suits with him. When I heard the name, I was shocked that this squared away Marine was the impersonator that I arrested.

The judge went through the normal procedure of asking if he wanted a jury trial, a postponement, or did he want to proceed with the trial today. The two guys in suits turned out to be his attorney and a doctor. His attorney said that his client would be pleading guilty. He asked the judge if he could speak on behalf of the Marine.

The judge accepted the guilty plea. I testified about the arrest. After I testified, the attorney said he had no questions for me. He proceeded to tell the judge about the Marine. He said that he had fourteen years in the Marine Corps and was currently stationed at Quantico, Virginia. He talked about his age, his education, his duty stations while in the Marines, and painted a picture of a pretty decent person.

He then told the judge that this Marine suffered from a condition that was not medical but was more mental. He asked the doctor to explain it to the judge. The doctor flat out stated that this Marine possessed a compulsion to dress like a female. He said that he has been treating the Marine for a couple of years and was working on the problem. The doctor testified that the Marine started by dressing around his home in woman's clothes. He then started to walk in his neighborhood late at night dressed as a female. He stated that the urge to dress like a female got intense and that is when he would travel to nearby cities and walk the streets.

As you can imagine, the courtroom was silent as everyone including the judge were mesmerized by the doctor's testimony. He went on to say that the Marine was not a homosexual and did not dress like a female for sex. He did come up with some medical terms that he said the Marine suffered from. The whole time the doctor was talking, the Marine stood tall and looked straight ahead at the judge.

When the doctor finished, the lawyer took over and asked that the judge give the Marine the benefit of the doubt and find him not guilty. He said that the incident had already been reported to the Marine Corps and he would probably be severely disciplined.

The judge leaned back in his chair and said he had never in his time on the bench come across anything like this. He asked the doctor to repeat what he thought was mentally wrong with the Marine.

The judge asked me if the Marine had given me a hard time when I arrested him and I said he did not. You could see that the judge was having a real dilemma about this case. The judge told the attorney that he really did not have much choice but to find the Marine guilty. He then paused and said, "Sergeant, because of your many years of service to our country, I'm going to give you probation before verdict. I'm going to stipulate that you will be on probation for one year. I sincerely hope that you get the help that you need."

Being a Marine myself, I left the courtroom feeling bad, knowing that this veteran Marine sergeant would most likely be dishonorably discharged from the Marine Corps.

I was leaving the building about the same time the Marine sergeant and his attorney were leaving. I was very much surprised when the Marine came over to me and said he appreciated my lenient testimony. I shook his hand and wished him well.

When he started to walk away, I told him that I was a Marine. He walked back and we shook hands again. As he was walking down the ramp of the station house, he turned and hollered to me, *"Semper Fi Marine!"*

Conversation # 6

When I joined the Baltimore City Police Department in 1965, we were not making much money. It was a lot more than the eighty-nine dollars I was getting monthly in the Marines. So, at first it seemed like I struck it rich. But when you're young, just married, and starting a family, a police paycheck at that time didn't go very far.

By 1969, I had four years on the job, two kids, and we were still not making much money. I would work overtime anytime I could to make a little extra. I was not alone in this endeavor; most cops I knew were in the same boat. It was not until much later in my career that the police department started to pay a halfway decent salary.

So, to help pay the bills, we worked overtime whenever we could. If you made an arrest, you would get paid to go to court on your off time. It wasn't much money for court appearance...we got three dollars for district court and five dollars for circuit court and that was not by the hour, that was for the entire day. Whenever the opportunity came up for making money, I would jump on it, like everyone else.

In 1969, the city was experiencing a rash of taxicab robberies. The Sun Cab company sought the help of the police department. If you would volunteer to drive a cab, the company would waive the daily rental of the cab, you would pay for the gas, and you would keep a large portion of the cab fares for the time you were on the street. The only stipulation was that they wanted you to work at night. I signed up to do this, figuring this would be an easy way to make some much-needed money.

I drove a cab for about two weeks and it seemed like it would be a piece of cake. I must admit that I learned early that you did not pick up suspicious looking characters. I guess the suspicious looking characters were probably the ones doing the robberies. I really wasn't out there to get robbed; I wanted to make some money.

Well, I picked up a couple one night a little after midnight. I picked them up near *The Block* in downtown Baltimore. It was a black man and a black woman. It was summertime, so when I looked them over, they appeared to be okay. I assumed that with the clothes they had on, they didn't have any weapons.

When they got in the cab, I could tell right away that they had been drinking. The guy told me they wanted to go to the nineteen hundred block of Fremont Avenue. When I heard that, I was thinking this ain't good. That area was a high crime area of the city. I was very familiar with that area since I had worked there in uniform at one time. I thought for a minute and decided to give it a shot.

As I was driving to that location, I kept watching them in the rear-view mirror. At first, they seemed to be fine, but as I approached Fremont Avenue, things started to change. I noticed the guy was appearing a little fidgety. Remember, I'm a cop by trade, not a cab driver, I pick these things up.

As I drove up Fremont Avenue, the guy said, "At the next little street, turn down there."

I told him that I would rather leave them out on Fremont Avenue. I pulled the cab over and told them what the fare showed. The guy started to argue with me and said, "I told you to go down that little street."

I told him I was not going to argue and that this is where they get out. He appeared to be going in a pocket, and then casually he said, "We ain't got no money, so we appreciate the ride."

He started to make a move to open the door. I pulled my gun and pointed it at him. I remember the incident like it was yesterday, I said, "You ain't going anywhere...I'm not a cab driver, I'm a police officer, and I want to get paid."

He was shocked to see my gun. He would have been even more shocked if he had known that I had another gun in an ankle holster. The female appeared to be a little shaken by my actions. She told me that if I would drive her to her mother's house, she would get the money. I knew I was not driving any further with these two. I asked them what they had on them that could pay for the taxi ride. They both looked at me and she said, "You mean you want our stuff?"

I said, "If you can't pay me with cash, I'll take whatever you have. You knew all this time that you didn't have any money. If I don't get paid, I'm going to lock you up for failing to pay a cab fare. So, it's either you pay me in cash or give me something of value. So, what's it going to be? I'm getting paid someway or you go to jail."

The guy started to reach for the door handle again. I told him he was making a big mistake. He smiled at me and said, "You mean you would shoot me over a cab ride?"

I felt the Clint Eastwood syndrome coming over me. I told him, "There is only one way to find out...just keep pulling that handle and we will see what happens."

I guess I got my point across. I got a watch from him and a bracelet from her. They got out of the cab and I got the hell out of that area as quick as I could.

If you're thinking at this point that I probably robbed them before they could rob me...you would be right. In a dangerous city like Baltimore, you don't wait for shit to happen, because it almost always does. I would not call this a robbery, I would put in the category of bartering.

I drove a cab for another couple of nights and quit. I could not get used to people sitting in the back seat where I could not see what they were doing. I decided that walking a beat on the dangerous streets of Baltimore City was much safer than driving a cab.

It has been many years since this incident happened, but I remember it well...do you think those two sit around and tell people about the night a police officer robbed them...excuse me, bartered with them.

Conversation # 7

In the late '60s I was working in the Central District Operations Squad. We worked in uniform and occasionally in plainclothes. I mentioned this in a prior conversation. The theory behind the Operations Unit was to work an area where there was a lot of crime. We would work in marked cars for prevention and in plainclothes sometimes to actually catch the bad guys. I can honestly say that other than working in the Central District Vice Unit, the Operations Unit was one of my favorite assignments.

The Central District had a lot of activity with its stores, restaurants, colleges, museums, railroad station, nightclubs, strip joints, the harbor, and much more. On any given day, when working in plainclothes we could find an area that presented a chance to make some arrests.

It could be the Maryland Avenue bridge to catch the bad guys breaking into vehicles owned by students attending the University of Baltimore. It could be just following junkies after they got their methadone from the clinic at Charles and 21st Street. It could be mixing in with the students at the Maryland Art Institute smoking marijuana on the grass outside the school. The possibilities went on and on; there was never a dull moment.

Our supervisor got a report that there were several street robberies occurring in an area off of Charles Street close to some of the high-dollar restaurants. When these street muggings happened, the victims were usually customers leaving a restaurant after enjoying a meal and a few drinks. They would get approached by a couple guys asking for directions and if the opportunity was right, they produced a weapon and robbed them. The only advantage we had in this situation, was that the assailants were black guys operating in an area mostly frequented at night by white people. The M.O. was the same. They would approach people walking to their cars on the smaller streets just off of Charles Street. The assailants would ask for directions, produce a gun and take wallets, watches, jewelry, and money. The reports of the robberies indicated that no one had been injured thus far.

My sergeant decided that we would flood the area in plainclothes in an effort to catch what appeared to be the same group doing the robberies. We worked in the area for two nights and didn't have any reports of a robbery. On the third night, my partner and I followed two very suspicious looking guys that were walking up and down Morton Street, which was a very small street between Charles Street and Cathedral Street. We decided to get a couple others in the squad to assist us with a plan to see if these guys were the culprits in the prior robberies.

After meeting for a few minutes, we decided to have one of us walk down Morton Street to see if the suspicious looking guys would approach us. At the time, the plan we came up with seemed to be no big deal, but looking back on it, it was kind of crazy. We decided that I would walk down the street pretending to be intoxicated. The other guys would be at both ends of the street in case I was approached. I did have my gun concealed, but as I was walking down the street, it hit me that maybe this time the bad guys might use their gun.

I added a little bait to the plan. I had my wallet out counting money as I staggered down the street. I know you're probably thinking, is this the dumbest thing ever and is it entrapment? The answer is yes to the dumbest thing and no to entrapment.

About halfway down the street, I was approached by two black guys. At first, one of them asked if they could help me to my car. I staggered some more, all the time watching any quick movements on their part. I was looking further down the street for my guys when my wallet was snatched out of my hand. It happened quick. I started chasing them and hollering *police*. They were running and weaving in and out of parked cars. When they got to Read Street, my guys stopped them without incident. We searched them and did not find a gun or my wallet. I asked where my wallet was. They said they didn't know what I was talking about. They said they were just walking down the street when I just started to chase them.

We arrested both of them and went to look for my wallet. Well, we not only found my wallet and we found a handgun. They apparently threw the wallet and their gun over a fence. I guess this is one of those times when you just thank your lucky stars.

When we went to court with these two guys, I testified just the way it happened. The defense attorney asked the judge to dismiss the case on the grounds of entrapment. The judge was a salty old guy who had been around for a long time. He told the attorney that he sometimes frequents that area and it could have been him getting robbed. He further stated that what I did was perfectly legal and no one forced them to rob me. The judge said that there was enough evidence to hold the two of them for trial in Circuit Court.

I've been involved in some dumb shit during my career, but looking back on it, this one ranks right up there...but I can't decide which is number one, there were so many.

Conversation # 8

As an Irishman from the great neighborhood of St. John's in East Baltimore or more formally known as the 10th Ward, I want to have this conversation with you about a St. Patrick's Day back in 1967.

I wrote about this neighborhood in my first book. It was the neighborhood I grew up in, went to school there, and walked a beat when I was a rookie cop. I don't want to slight any other neighborhood in Baltimore City, but this one was the greatest.

Even today when you meet people from the city, you always ask them where they grew up. It's sort of like when you ask someone what high school they attended. There are a lot of great old neighborhoods in the city, but I don't know of any that still have an organization named after the neighborhood. I am still a member and we proudly call the group...*St. John's – Tenth Ward Oldtimers.* It's a club with officers, dues paying members, and yearly events. You can't go anywhere in the city without someone saying they are from the Tenth Ward. I know the boundaries of the Tenth Ward and some are not telling the truth...but, that's okay, if they want to be a proud Irishman from the Tenth Ward, that's fine.

As an Irishman, I try to attend all the St. Patrick's Day parades. On that day, you can walk up and down the parade route with a beer in your hand and the cops say nothing. I remember the days when certain bars would have very large crowds out in front of their place...extending a couple of blocks down the street.

A few that come to mind over the years are: Bernie Lee's Pub, Kavanaugh's, The Stil, Jerry D's, The Shamrock, and the Emerald Tavern. I know I have visited some of these bars on St. Patrick's Day and the celebration would go on late into the night and sometimes into the early hours of the next day.

There is no other ethnic group that celebrates its heritage better than the Irish. It doesn't matter what your name is or where your family came from, on St. Patrick's Day everyone is Irish. Where else would you go to see a river turned green on that day or the streets painted green? If you've never been to an Irish bar on St. Patrick's Day, you need to put that on your bucket list.

The conversation that I want to talk about with you occurred on St. Patrick's Day, March 17, 1967.

I was working the 4 P.M. to midnight shift in the Central District. I was in uniform and working in a marked police car. It was a nice day and all the bars started the celebration as soon as they opened in the early morning.

I was patrolling around Charles and Read streets when a Rolls-Royce flew by me at a high rate of speed. I got behind the Rolls and watched the car go through the red lights at Eager Street, Chase Street, Biddle Street and Preston Street. I could not believe that anyone would be that brazen knowing a cop car with flashing lights and siren was right behind them. Also, this was a very busy part of town with a large amount of pedestrian traffic.

I requested from the police dispatcher to have a patrol car attempt to block the Rolls around Mount Royal Avenue. I was told that the car had already passed Mount Royal and was approaching the entrance to the Jones Falls Expressway which leads you North and out of the city.

I accelerated and could see the Rolls taking that exit onto the expressway. I finally got behind the Rolls and it was apparent that the driver had no intentions of stopping. When we approached the Cold Spring Lane exit, the Rolls pulled to the shoulder...only because several other police cars had joined the chase.

What happened next is something I will never forget. I walked up to the driver side of the car. I could see that there were seven people in the car. Along with the driver, there were two females in the front. In the back I saw four people, two females and two males. Even with a good size vehicle like a Rolls, the people in the back were crunched in. I waited for the driver to roll down the window and as I waited, I could hear all the passengers laughing. I also noticed that the group in the back were drinking beer and something else in cups.

When the driver rolled down the window, the smell of smoke and alcohol were permeating from the car. Before I could say anything, the driver said, "Officer, how long is this going to take? We got a party to go to!"

I didn't immediately respond to him, but I was thinking to myself...*you are hardly going to make your party.*

I told him that I had observed him running several red lights on Charles Street at a high rate of speed. I asked for his license and registration. The conversation got even better at this point. I could tell by his slurred speech that he was intoxicated. He was fumbling through his wallet and dropping things on his lap. He said, "I don't know if I have my license with me. Can you just write the tickets and I'll be on my way?"

All the time I was talking with this guy, the rest of the passengers were laughing and having a good old time. Finally, he found his license and registration and handed them to me. When I took the cards, I found a hundred-dollar bill in between the license and the registration card. Being young and maybe a little naïve, I said, "Your money was stuck between your cards."

I tried to hand him the hundred-dollar bill back. He then said with a silly laugh, "That's yours officer, I'm a real supporter of cops."

I was thinking fast and I knew that this was a bribe to just let him go. I'm not sure where I came up with the idea, but I asked him to initial the hundred-dollar bill. He laughed and said, "If that's what it takes, no problem, I just want to be on my way."

He initialed the money and handed it back to me. I asked him to get out of the car. He at first laughed, but did get out. By this time, several other officers were on the scene. I told him he was under arrest for numerous traffic violations, driving intoxicated, and for bribing a police officer. I turned him around on his car and put handcuffs on him. He was mumbling all kinds of nasty talk to me. When I was waiting for the police wagon to transport him to the district, he had the nerve to say, "Listen officer, you don't know me, but my dad owns one of the biggest construction companies in Maryland. He knows all the judges in this city and you locking me up will go nowhere. If you just need a little more money, just let me know...whatever it takes and I can be on my way."

I won't mention his full name. He was Polish and his name ended in "Ski", so I will call him Ski in this conversation. I did find out later that his dad was very wealthy.

Ski was taken to the district and was charged with all the traffic violations...reckless driving, speeding, DUI, and bribing a police officer. The car was towed because I did not think anyone in the vehicle was capable of driving. Someone in the car made a call and they were all picked up. I assume they made the party...without Ski.

Ski made bail before all the paperwork was even done. He also had called his attorney. I was finishing my reports when my sergeant told me that a lawyer was in the building and asked to talk to me. I walked to the public area and saw a lawyer that I was familiar with. I had some cases with him in the past. His name was Tom Maxwell.

I had a lot of respect for this lawyer. He was a well-dressed, mild-mannered, and respected lawyer. When I had cases in court with him, he was always straight forward, never trying to discredit you. We were not friends, but whenever I saw him in court or on the street, he made it a point to talk to me. He greeted me this time when I approached him, the same way as always. He asked how I was doing, how was my family, and he was overly friendly.

He asked if there was somewhere private we could talk. We went in the roll call room. He wasted no time in getting to what he wanted to say.

"You arrested a very good client of mine and a personal friend. I have known him and his family for many years. His dad owns one of the largest construction companies in the state. He is very wealthy. What I would like to ask you is...would you consider going light on him with your testimony at the trial?"

He paused. I told him that what Ski had done was very serious. I went over the entire event with him. I told him that people could have been seriously injured by the way he was driving. I went on to tell him that after I stopped him, he thought the incident was funny. I said that at the trial, I will testify exactly the way it happened and no more. Mr. Maxwell got up from the chair. He reached to shake my hand and said, "I would hope you would think it over; there might be something in it for you."

I kind of knew what he was referring to, but I didn't respond. He pulled out his wallet and gave me his calling card. He said, "If you change your mind, give me a call."

I'm going to get right to the trial for Ski. The trial was held in the Central District Court and the presiding judge was, Judge Finnerty.

As some of the cases were being tried, I noticed Mr. Maxwell walking around the courtroom talking with other lawyers. I remember that when the judge first came onto the bench, the first person he said good morning to was Mr. Maxwell.

When my case was called to the bench, Judge Finnerty had a short conversation with Mr. Maxwell. You would have thought these two were at a bar having drinks. The judge asked him how his family was and they talked for a few minutes. I knew right away that I probably had an uphill battle to get a conviction on these charges.

I testified and probably talked for at least ten minutes. When I got to the part about pursuing Ski speeding up Charles Street and running the red lights, I noticed that the judge looked at Mr. Maxwell and smiled. I also noticed that the judge seemed to be fidgeting with some papers. He was not even looking at me while I was talking.

I finished testifying and the judge asked Mr. Maxwell if he had any questions for me. Maxwell asked some questions that seemed very pedestrian for such serious charges. He asked: if anyone was injured on Charles Street, if I saw any alcohol in his client's hand, if Ski gave me a hard time, and then he asked if I had ever met Ski before. I answered no to all the questions. I was kind of wondering why he asked if I had ever met his client before.

At this point, the judge told me that I had presented a good case against Ski. He asked Mr. Maxwell if he wanted to say anything on behalf of his client before he rendered a decision. Maxwell thanked the judge and started a spiel that went on for at least fifteen minutes. He painted Ski as this really great guy, a hard-working man, a guy that loves to have fun, a pillar in the community...and each time he said something, he would put his hand on Ski's shoulder.

The final blow came when he told the judge that it was St. Patrick's Day, a day of celebration for Irish people...(do you remember when I told you Ski was Polish), a day that most people in Baltimore go out and have a few drinks, and that is what Ski and his friends were doing. He went on to say that no one was hurt on Charles Street, no vehicles were damaged and his client did not give the officer any problems. The best part came when Maxwell said the hundred-dollar bill was just stuck between Ski's license and registration. He said Ski had no intentions of trying to bribe the officer. He finished by saying that his client smiles all the time and it was no disrespect toward the officer.

The judge was still fidgeting with papers but looked up when Maxwell stopped talking. I must say that at this point, I was thinking about the conversation I had with Mr. Maxwell when he told me to think it over about how I would testify. I was young and fairly new on the job, but I could figure it out that Maxwell had gotten to the judge. It couldn't be anymore clearer about what was about to happen.

Judge Finnerty put down the papers and looked directly at me with that big red face. He said, "Officer, you did a good job and you presented your case well. However, after hearing Mr. Maxwell talk about his client, I don't think he's a bad person. After all, it was St. Patrick's Day (remember the name...Judge Finnerty) ...and maybe he did have a few drinks too many, but nobody got hurt. I feel that Mr. Ski has learned a very valuable lesson from this incident. He's a hard-working man and I know that because I know his father. I don't think the hundred dollars was actually a bribe. If he would have said, Officer, this is for you to let me go, that would be different (actually he did say that) ...so under these circumstances and the fact that he has only had one prior minor arrest, I'm going to give him the benefit of the doubt. I will render a verdict of not guilty on all charges."

As soon as I heard the words, *not guilty*, I turned and walked toward the door. Apparently, the judge was not done with me. He shouted to the rear of the courtroom, "Officer, come back up here for a minute."

I walked back to the bench and figured he would berate me for walking away. He told Mr. Maxwell and Ski that they could leave the courtroom. He then told me to come in his chambers. I figured...oh shit, I'm in trouble now, how will I handle this. After taking off his robe, the judge sat in his chair. He told me to sit down; he wanted to tell me something.

He went on to say that he knew my father...*my father was a cop for thirty years and knew a lot of people, including judges.*

He said, "I see a lot of your father in you and that's a good thing. I don't want you to be upset about my decision in your case. I base my decisions on a lot of factors. It's not easy being a judge. I have to do what is in the best interest of all parties. You did a good job and I'm sure you will continue to be a good cop, so don't be down over one court decision." He stood and shook my hand and said, "Tell your dad I said hello."

While driving home I ran it all through my head…Mr. Maxwell surely got to the judge. The night Maxwell met me in the station house he wanted me to take some money for a lenient testimony at the trial.

I remember later talking to an old-time sergeant about what happened. I will always remember his very wise wisdom, his advice, his deep thoughts about what I told him and just an overall great learning experience when he said, **"You dumb shit, you should have taken the money."**

Conversation # 9

Remember earlier when I told you I couldn't swim? I still can't, so this conversation should really amuse you.

I had been transferred from the Central District to the Northeast District in 1970. I had arrested a couple hundred people who were in an illegal nightclub. The judge who tried the case didn't like my testimony in court. He called the police commissioner and I was transferred. If you want that whole story, you will need to get my first book, *Cop Stories-The Few, The Proud, The Ugly.*

I was in the Northeast District during the winter of 1971. I was working a patrol car around the old Memorial Stadium on 33rd Street. I got a call to respond to Montebello Lake which was just off of 33rd Street and Hillen Road.

To say it was cold that night would not do it justice. I think the temperature was in the single digits. I was working the 4 P.M. to midnight shift and everything had been fairly quiet. When you have single digit weather, the streets are usually bare. Most of the crime in that kind of weather is on the inside.

I was relaxing with a cup of coffee when I got the call that a dog had wandered onto the frozen water of Montebello Lake. The lake and the adjoining filtration plant were the second largest in the country when they were built. The lake was a focal point when giving directions to people looking for Memorial Stadium. The water in the lake ran from the Loch Raven Reservoir in Baltimore County to Montebello Lake, which is a mind-boggling feat in itself, as they are many miles apart from each other.

The surrounding area of the lake also served another very important mission...it served as a parking place for lovers. On any given night, you could ride around the lake and when you looked into the parked cars, you very seldom saw two heads. The cops that worked the area had taught me a trick that they had been using for years. When you would drive by the parked car, you could shine your flashlight at the parked car window and it acted as a mirror...you could see everything.

Some nights there were so many parked cars that the number of cop cars driving around outnumbered the parked cars. When the procedure didn't reveal any bodies in the car, you would have to stop and check it out. You would be amazed how low two people in the front seat of a car can get. If you think the cops were weird dudes when looking in the parked cars...you're right, but it's cold outside and nothing better to do.

Now back to the conversation about the dog stuck on the ice. When I got to the lake, you could see the dog and he seemed like he was exactly in the middle of the lake. He had apparently wandered onto the lake and hit a soft spot and fell through. He had his front legs up on the ice and the rest was in the frigid water. A few other cop cars had pulled up to the scene when they heard the call. We were standing around when the lieutenant arrived. We were thinking about trying to slide out on the ice to get the dog. The spot where the dog was, in the center of the lake, was about the distance of a football field.

The lieutenant called for the emergency wagon. This unit carried all kinds of tools and equipment for whatever emergency would come up. The unit actually had a small boat on board. The boat was put on the ice and two guys got in the boat with an ax and they looked like George Washington crossing the Delaware. Well, that didn't work, as the ice was thick. It actually looked like the ice was freezing up as quick as they were trying to chop at it.

After about a half hour, it was obvious the dog was in dire distress. A crowd started to gather at the lake. People were parking their cars and offering all kinds of suggestions on how to get the dog. Finally, the lieutenant had a brilliant idea or at least he thought so...that's why they get the big bucks. He called for the police helicopter. His plan was to tie a rope around the skids of the helicopter and someone could hold the rope, walk across the lake, and rescue the dog.

The emergency unit did have a long strong rope. After communicating with the helicopter pilot, everything was in place...except the part about who was walking across the lake to get the dog. I was standing there minding my business when I saw the lieutenant looking at me. He said, "Officer Ellwood, you look about the right size to give this a try."

At first, I thought he was kidding, but he walked over to me and put his hand on my shoulder...I felt like he was a mafia hit-man putting the death curse on me.

The other cops were egging me on, only because they wanted no part of this crazy idea.

Well, being a Marine and gung-ho and all that other bullshit that goes along with being a Marine, I said I would do it. The helicopter was flying over the lake to see if their blades would crack the ice. The chopper than landed on a grassy spot and the helicopter observer was given the rope. The sound of the chopper was deafening and it was blowing up everything around us. Along with the temperature in single digits, the chopper blades made it feel even colder. We were communicating with the pilot to let him know that when he dropped the rope, I would tie it around my chest under my arms and we would be set to go. I took off most of my equipment. I put on a knit hat and was ready to go.

The chopper appeared to be about fifty feet over our heads. The force of the downdraft of the blades made me use all the strength I had to just stay on my feet. When I started to walk on the ice, it was the weirdest thing I had ever done. I'm not sure if my feet were even touching the ice...I think I was being dragged across the ice.

When I got to the dog, it appeared that he was using all his strength to stay afloat. I'm not a dog lover, but I felt bad for this guy. I'm not sure what he was thinking, but as I got closer, he appeared to struggle more to get on the ice. While trying to stay erect on the ice, I reached down and with my first grab, I got hold of the dog's collar strap. I was lucky to get it on the first try and so was the dog. I tried to lift him out of the water, but his soaked body was extremely heavy. I finally managed to get him on the ice and the chopper headed back to the shoreline. When I got closer, the guys in the boat grabbed the dog. I was literally dropped onto the grassy area as I let go of the rope. I watched the chopper go airborne and disappear with the rope still hanging from the bottom.

The people on the grass had some blankets and wrapped the dog in them. I wasn't as wet as the dog, but I sure as hell could have used a blanket. I sat in the car with the heater running and thawed out. I still had a few hours left on my shift. The lieutenant came over to my car and thanked me. He told me to take the car into the station and go home.

I found out later that the dog was taken to an animal hospital by some people who had gathered to watch the rescue.

When I went home that night, my wife asked why I was home early and why were my pants and shoes so wet.

I told her the story and she said, "You can't swim. What if the ice would have cracked?"

After warming up, I did think about what would have happened if things went wrong. I guess the dog would have drowned, I could have drowned, the helicopter could have crashed, and probably that lieutenant would have been fired for coming up with the dumbest plan that only a young police officer would go along with.

I guess the rescue of this dog makes up for the story in my first book where I had to shoot a dog my first day on the job.

Conversation # 10

I have written a lot about walking a foot post in the neighborhood that I grew up in. I have also written about cops not having much equipment back in those days, like a police radio, handcuffs, extra bullets, and we even had to buy our shirts. Seeing what cops are equipped with today is amazing. Regardless of the equipment and the working conditions, I can tell you that some of my greatest memories on the police department come from walking a beat in the neighborhood I grew up in.

Having joined the police department right out of the Marine Corps was a real eye-opener for me. I was used to discipline, comradery, teamwork, and a spirit of everyone working together for the same goal. Some of the supervisors in the police department back then had only certain things in mind...put in their eight hours, make sure they got fed, maybe have a few drinks while they were working, and take home whatever wasn't nailed down.

If I were to compare a sergeant in the police department with a sergeant in the Marine Corps...there would be no comparison. Some supervisors in the police department back then, couldn't last a day in the Marines. I did say some...there were many others that were good supervisors; I just didn't have them early in my career.

Let me tell you about my first supervisor in the police department, Sergeant George Capp. We could have a really long conversation about this guy. What I'm going to tell you could be verified by any cop that worked for Sergeant Capp back in those days. Sergeant Capp had to have paid for his stripes; no way in hell did he earn them by being a good police officer. When I say, paid for his stripes, it's no secret that way back when my dad was a cop, you could buy a promotion if you knew the right people. I don't remember the exact money that was needed, but in today's world, it would be chump change. I had heard many conversations amongst my dad's cop friends on who they knew had paid for their promotion.

I actually think my dad was approached to buy his stripes, but he either didn't have the money, which is most likely when you have six kids, or he was very happy being a traffic cop. My dad loved being around people and directing traffic in downtown Baltimore gave him that opportunity.

Let's get back to Sergeant Capp and his disgusting ways that he supervised cops. Let me start by saying it was known that he was a big drinker, both on and off the job. I knew of many times when he came to work and you could tell he had been drinking. He made no bones about it and the shift lieutenants knew it but didn't care to do anything about it. My guess is that they didn't really give a shit as long as he could make it to his bailiwick, last eight hours, go through the motions of being a supervisor, and simply do not cause any problems for them.

Sergeant Capp was a short man. He was not by any means your poster guy...not even close. He usually showed up for work with a not so clean uniform. He smoked and had that gruff cancer voice. I can remember times when he would not even remember your name. For a long time in his squad, I thought my name was "boy" ...it was hey boy, do this boy, come with me boy, where you been boy, don't bother me boy, and every time he called me boy, I wanted to say, "Hey, you piece of shit, I ain't no fuckin boy. I just put four years in the Marine Corps and they don't produce boys, they produce men."

I could have many conversations with you about Sergeant Capp, but I will stick with one that still bothers me today. When you worked on any shift with him, usually about two hours into the shift, you knew he had been drinking. You could smell it on his breath, his demeanor changed, he got nasty, and sometimes he even staggered.

In those days, we had to write reports while we were in the field. We would either carry some reports with us or have a business place that we could go and write the report. After you would write the report, you took it to the sergeant for his approval. In Sergeant Capp's case you would have to find the bar he was in. When you found him, you had to gently approach him. Most of the time he was sitting right at the bar as if he were a patron and he was in full police uniform. When you approached him, his first statement would be, "What the fuck you bothering me for now, boy?"

He would take the report and pretend he was reading it and throw it back at you...that meant he approved. Sometimes when he was drunk, he would tear it up and then throw it at you and say, "This looks like shit, write it over and stop bothering me, boy."

Well, I'm sure you have a mental picture of what a total jerk this guy was. One night just as it was getting dark, I got a call for a domestic disturbance. I went to the house and the husband and wife were going at it pretty good. When I walked in, they kept right on screaming at each other as if I was not even there.

I'll tell you now that these kinds of calls can turn out to be very dangerous. You can imagine when a husband and wife are arguing, the last thing they want to see is a twenty-two-year old cop come in their home and tell them why they should stop fighting. In some cases, you have to ask one of them to leave the house for a while and that was my strategy that night.

In this case, the husband was the aggressor. I asked him to take a walk and cool off. He was shouting at me and told me to get out of his house...he actually screamed it in some nasty language. I was trying to be calm, but he was getting to me. He finally walked toward the front door. He turned, ran back in the living room and struck his wife in the face. I grabbed him, subdued him and put my handcuffs on him. Remember...we were all walking in those days and you were pretty much on your own in situations like this. I started out of the house with him and he was not cooperating at all. I knew I had to walk this guy about three blocks to the call box to get the wagon to respond and take him to the station.

The call box had a phone in it and was our connection to the police dispatcher. The guy I was arresting was about my size, but when you're trying to literally carry someone that has been drinking...they feel like dead weight. When someone is resisting, they know what they're doing and you do not.

I was about one block from the call box and this guy had calmed down a little. You had to use a little psychology in those days when talking to someone as pissed off as he was. While holding on to this guy and feeling good about almost making it to the call box...things changed.

I heard Sergeant Capp walk up behind me and say, "What the fuck did this nigger do?" (I only use this word to give you the full effect of what was happening).

As you can imagine, I now had my prisoner struggling again...not so much toward me, but toward Capp. He was trying to get to Capp and I could feel the strength back in his struggling. We got to the call box and I called for the wagon. For the next ten minutes, it was a verbal battle back and forth between Capp and my prisoner. I will not go into the language that Capp used...I'm sure you can only imagine. When the wagon arrived, I walked my guy to the back and the two of them were still screaming at each other. I wanted to tell Capp to shut the fuck up, but being new and with people around, I didn't do it.

As the officer working the wagon was helping my prisoner into the wagon, Capp hit the guy on the leg with his nightstick for no apparent reason. The prisoner was furious and tried to get at Capp who was about ready to hit him again. I had seen enough and told Capp to back off. It was not necessary to be hitting a handcuffed prisoner. Well, Capp looked at me and started to rip me apart verbally. As the door was about to be closed on the wagon, Capp kept screaming the "N" word at the guy. It was embarrassing because a crowd had gathered around to watch the action.

I can remember the last exchange between the two of them. Capp called the guy the "N" word and the prisoner called Capp a fuckin drunk. Still not letting up, Capp shouted to the guy, "I might be a drunk, but tomorrow I'll be sober and you'll still be a fuckin nigger." (I apologize for using that word, but I again want to paint a picture of what an asshole Capp was).

You know, all things come to shitheads in due time...not really a saying, but I'm using it just the same. About twelve years after this incident, I was working in the Homicide Unit. We naturally handled all homicides, but we also handled serious shootings and suicides.

We got a call from the dispatcher that a uniform officer wanted a detective to respond to his location for a suicide. My partner, Frank Perkowski and I took the assignment. We went to a house in the Hamilton section of Northeast Baltimore. When we got there, the uniform officer told us that the suicide attempt was on a retired Baltimore police officer. The ambulance had responded and took the man to the hospital. The officer was not sure if the man had died, but he did have a self-inflicted gunshot wound to the head. The home we were in was filthy and liquor bottles were all over the kitchen and some just lying on the living room floor. We were told that this man lived alone.

We went to Union Memorial Hospital's emergency room. We knew some of the nurses from prior visits to the ER. We went back to where our suicide guy was and found out from the nurse that he did not die in his attempt to take his life. He did have a gunshot wound to the head and was being treated by the staff.

We waited outside the treating room until it was determined if we would be able to talk to him. We were going over the admitting papers on this guy and when I saw his name...I screamed pretty loud, "Holy shit, it's George Capp!"

My partner was telling me to hold it down; we're in a hospital. I waved the paperwork at him, "You don't understand. It's Sergeant George Capp...the piece of shit that I worked for when I was a rookie on the job."

I was pacing the hallway, just waiting for the word from the nurse that we could see Capp. We were told that he would survive his gunshot wound, but would be admitted to the hospital. I was chomping at the bit to see this asshole. When the nurse said we could go in his cubicle, I walked toward his bed. All I saw was a very old and frail man with his head wrapped in bandages.

I stood right over him and a weird thought came over me...*how pitiful this man looked*. The same man that treated people like dirt many years ago was now just a sad old man that tried to take his life. I just wanted to get the information I needed and get the hell out of there.

Before I could say anything, he looked up at me and said, "What the fuck do you want?"

Well, now...here we are these many years later and my old sergeant is talking to me just like he did when I was a rookie. The only difference this time is: I'm in charge, I'm asking the questions, I'm standing over a man that is still a real piece of shit and the best part is that I don't feel sorry for him...not at all.

I tried to be professional and asked Mr. Capp what happened. Well, he commenced to use the only language he knew...fuck, fuck, fuck and fuck. I stopped him and said, "Mr. Capp, did you try to commit suicide?"

He tried to roll his head toward me and said, "You cops today don't know shit...you damn right I tried to kill myself. I guess I didn't do a good job, because I'm still here talking to you assholes."

I knew we were going nowhere with Mr. Capp. I just wanted to say one thing to him before we left. He was mumbling something and giving the nurse a hard time. I leaned over facing him and said, "Mr. Capp, I know you don't remember me. I worked in your squad when I was a rookie. I'm sorry you tried to end your life. This might not be the appropriate time to tell you, but you are the most miserable human being I have ever come across. I hope, while you now have a second chance at life, you make some changes. The way you treated me and other young cops way back, made us want to be better people. We all knew that by watching you day after day, there was no way in hell we wanted to turn out like you."

My partner and I left his room. We were walking to our car when Frank said, "Damn, you really laid it on that old bastard."

I stopped and touched Frank's arm, "Frank, we just talked to a man that by the way he lived his life, he touched many people. The cops that turned out good, did not want to be like him and the cops that turned out bad, were bad because of him."

While walking to the car, I had a final thought about Mr. Capp. I was thinking that I should have told him that the next time he contemplated killing himself, hold the gun a little more steadier and get the job done.

I'm sure my old sergeant has passed on by now. In a way, a morbid kind of way, I probably owe him something. Watching him be the way he was on a daily basis, made me want to be a good police officer, and more than that, a good person.

Conversation # 11

There are times when just because you're a police officer your neighbors or friends think you need to take action. This conversation is about one of those times.

I can remember as a young kid growing up my dad would be called upon in our neighborhood to handle something just because he was a cop.

Back when my three sisters, my two brothers and I were young, it was not unusual for people to come to our house in the evening seeking advice or a favor from my dad. He had a lot of connections, but most of all he had common sense. He knew where to direct people who had some type of problem. It could be a city service that they needed, it court be a problem with someone in the neighborhood, it could be a traffic or parking ticket, it could be a domestic problem, and the list goes on and on. It seemed like he could not turn anyone away. If he didn't have a solution for them, he would know someone that could help them. He never tried to avoid any of the neighbors that came to our house.

Another thing he inherited by being a cop, was the call to go to homes where someone had just died. The doorbell would ring in the early morning hours and a neighbor would ask my dad to come to their home...a relative had passed away. He would get dressed and out the door he would go. It wasn't that our neighbors couldn't handle these types of things. It was that my dad was a cop...and everyone back them looked up to the cops that lived in their neighborhood.

When dad would go to a home where a man had died, it would not be unusual to see him weeks later wearing the deceased man's suit. His friends always would kid him when they saw him with a new suit or some other new clothing.

Back in those days, the neighbors all knew each other. When someone was sick, neighbors would make sure they took food to the home. When someone passed away, the neighbors rallied around the family.

We did have funeral parlors back then, but it seemed that they would just handle getting the casket and the flowers. Those that died in our neighborhood, were laid out in their living room and that's where the viewing took place. You always knew when someone had died, there was a large wreath on the front door.

As our neighborhood was mostly made up of Irish people, they had what they called an Irish wake. After the viewing at night, the men in the neighborhood would stay back in the living room and drink beer and whiskey. Some of these wakes went on until the sun came up the next day. It's a known fact that at most of the wakes, each person would talk about the deceased as if they were alive. I have heard that on occasion, they would lift the deceased out of the casket, place him in a chair and continue talking about him as if he were alive. I guess when morning came, they just put him back in the casket and went home.

Fast forward this conversation many years later when I was the cop in my neighborhood. Things were a little different, but I was also called upon many times to answer questions about some of the same things my dad had been asked. I'm not sure what the mystique is about being a cop...it seems that your neighbors feel safer that you're close by. I just can't imagine any other profession where someone would seek you out to answer legal questions or just ask for your help.

Even today when I'm retired from the police department, people still ask my opinion on something they may have read in the paper or something in the national news. I'm always careful responding because it just leads to more questions. Sometimes people don't want to hear what I really feel about certain incidents, especially when it involves a situation where they think a police officer was wrong.

I want to tell you about an incident that occurred in my neighborhood when my kids were very young. We lived in a nice neighborhood of townhouses. It's funny how the name of houses went from row houses when I was young, to townhouses when I got older. We liked the area and we got along with most neighbors. I think when your kids are young, you might sometimes have a little beef about something a neighbor doesn't like that your child did.

We had a neighbor that lived three doors down from our house. On the surface, they appeared to be fine. They had two kids that were about the same age as mine. The kids played in the alley in the rear of our homes. The father's name was Mike and the mother's name was Sue. I was never really sure what Mike did for employment, but I think he worked in a hospital.

Whenever I was out back with the kids, he made it a point to come out and talk to me. The conversation always dealt with police work. Mike told me that he tried to get on the police department but was turned down. I never asked why he was turned down, but I kind of think it had to do with his weight; he was very heavy. It may also have had something to with his mental state…. he was very flaky.

I think from talking to him and hearing bits and pieces from other neighbors, Mike, may have been experiencing some financial problems. Sue didn't work and Mike worked at the hospital and we later found out that he took a second job as a security guard.

Well, here's the part that I want to get to. I was sitting in my house and we were having dinner with the kids. Everything was peaceful and we were discussing what the kids had been doing that day. In the middle of our talk, I heard banging on my back door. I mean someone was beating the hell out of the door.

I ran to the door and it was Sue. She was crying and trying to tell me something, but it just wasn't coming out legible. I told her to calm down and tell me what was wrong. She came in our house and told me that Mike was sitting in the kitchen and was talking about killing himself. She said her kids were at her mother's house. She said that when Mike came home from work, she could tell something was wrong. He sat in the kitchen and was just mumbling over and over that he was a failure. She said that she tried to calm him down, but it got worse. He went to their bedroom and got a gun. He told her to leave the house, he didn't want to kill himself in front of her. I asked her if she had called the police and she said no. She said that he begged her not to call the police, because that would only make things worse. I asked her if she really believed he would kill himself. She said that he has talked about it in the past and obviously has never followed through.

I was about to call the county police when Sue begged me not to. She said, "If you go over and talk to him, he will put the gun away…he respects you."

Well, if you're thinking that I'm going to tell you that I agreed to go over and talk to him...you would be correct. Not sure what I was thinking, but I went over to his back door. I hollered his name and got no response. I opened the door and kept saying his name. Finally, I could see him in the kitchen at the table. I think I probably said something like, "Hey Mike, what's going on buddy?"

He did look up at me and that's when I saw the gun in his hand. I started talking and I'm not sure what I even said to him, but he seemed to be listening. I didn't want to ask for the gun just yet. I was hoping I could gain some ground by just talking. Whatever I said, he would respond and did not appear to be delusional. After a while, I asked for the gun and he didn't answer me. I figured I would talk about his kids and what the affect would be on them if he killed himself. I told him that no matter what his problems were, they could be worked out.

We must have talked for at least thirty minutes. I was getting a little worried that I couldn't get the gun away from him. I know this will sound a little crazy, but I actually had the thought to get tough with him. I felt like saying, *Mike, if you're really going to shoot yourself, why don't you do it in the bathroom. If you shoot yourself here in the kitchen, it's going to be one hell of a mess. You don't want your kids to come home and find your brains all over the kitchen floor.*

Don't jump ahead of me on this conversation...I didn't say that to him. I did tell him that I was leaving because I had things to do with my kids. He asked me not to leave. He pushed the gun across the table and started to cry. I picked up the gun which was a five-shot revolver and was fully loaded. I emptied the cylinder and put the bullets in my pocket.

He got up from the table and thanked me for coming over. He said he was embarrassed. I told him that he really needed to make an appointment with someone that he can talk to about his problems. He promised me he would do that. I started to leave and he asked if he could come over my house for a while. I knew this was not a good idea and I told him so. I asked if I could hold onto the gun until he made arrangements to get some counseling.

We talked his wife into returning home. She agreed that she would make sure they followed up with the counseling.

When I got back home, the kids asked where I had been. I told them that I was talking to Mr. Mike. I then proceeded to have two of the strongest gin and tonics I have ever had.

I look back on that night and think about what could have gone wrong. He could have killed himself and taken me with him. I actually tried to avoid him after that incident. I'm sure the incident was embarrassing to him. I didn't want to talk about it and I'm not sure if he ever sought any counseling.

I think it was months later we found out that he had lost his job at the hospital. He had been arrested for stealing drugs. I know he went to court because he actually had the nerve to ask me if I would testify on his behalf.

I could just imagine my testimony, *Yes, your honor, I know Mr. Mike. He is an outstanding member of society, but he did try to kill himself one time."*

My dad handled a lot of problems in the old neighborhood when I was young, but I don't think he could top this story.

Hell, he would have told Mike to just kill himself. He would than grab a couple of nice suits and be on his way. I think the suits would have been too big for dad.

Conversation # 12

Let me throw out one more conversation about another neighbor.

In 1976, I moved my family from Baltimore County to Carroll County. The move was to relocate to an area that had some ground where the kids could roam around without getting hit by a car or run over by a trash truck. We searched different areas and found a very nice home in Carroll County.

I was working in the Homicide Unit at the time, which was located in the headquarters building in downtown Baltimore City. The drive from the new house to work was about thirty-four miles one way. At the time we purchased the house that didn't seem like a problem. The drive would be through some beautiful tree-lined backroads which had a lot of farms and looked very peaceful. I have to admit that over time, the ride got to be a real pain in the ass.

So, we moved to the new house, registered the kids in the local school, and things seemed like it would be just what the doctor ordered. The home was on a half acre, which was plenty of room for us. It would require cutting more grass and much more upkeep of the property. The homes were in a nice development and they were not that far apart. The kids quickly made some new friends and could easily walk to the neighbors' homes.

Here's the neighbor story:

My closest neighbor was a professor at Towson State College. He was a very nice guy that lived in his home with his wife. I remember that he kept his property immaculate...which I can't say I did. He was a young guy and this was their first home. He was friendly to a fault. Whenever I was outside, he made it a point to come over and engage me in conversation. I can explain this guy by saying that he was a nerd, a good nerd, but nevertheless a nerd. When he found out that I was a police officer, he did what most people did...ask about the crime problem in Baltimore City. He would question me on stuff he read in the newspaper. I don't think he agreed with much that I told him. Because he was a professor, I always had the feeling that I was being tested by this guy.

When I worked daywork, my neighbor and I would leave our houses about the same time. We would wave to each other as we pulled out of our driveways.

We took the same route every day. He was going to Towson and I was going into Baltimore City. So, for about twenty miles we would be heading in the same direction. The roads were narrow in some spots, but for the most part the main road was one way in each direction. On any given morning, he could be in back of me or I could be in back of him.

On this particular morning I was following him down the road. I remember that it was a little foggy out and had rained the night before. The road we traveled went through some very dense wooded areas on each side of the road. It would be no surprise to see deer along the wooded area or even crossing the road. The road we were on was Falls Road, which would lead us both to our destinations.

About ten minutes into the ride, I saw my neighbor's vehicle strike a deer. He almost lost control of the car. He managed to pull to the side of the road. I was so close behind him that I actually saw when he hit the deer. I could see the deer lying in the grass on the side of the road. I pulled over behind my neighbor's car and put on my flashing lights.

I probably should have mentioned this sooner, I was driving an unmarked police car. The police vehicle was not assigned to me. It was a vehicle used by homicide detectives on a daily basis. No one in the Homicide Unit had a vehicle assigned to them, except the captain. I had taken the vehicle home the night before, because I worked late and knew I had to be back to work in the morning. I was well aware that other detectives in the unit had done the same thing I did under the same circumstances.

I got out of my car and could see that my neighbor was extremely upset. He showed me where the deer was lying in the grass on the side of the road. I could tell that the deer was not dead but was in real distress. I think that his legs were broken, along with other injuries. My neighbor came over to me and asked me to shoot the deer to take it out of its misery. I was thinking that this would be the best thing for the deer and we could both be on our way. I told him that I wasn't sure if that was a legal thing to do. My neighbor then asked if I would call the county police and ask if they would respond.

I was thinking...*I can't shoot this deer and I can't use the police radio to call for assistance.*

65

I knew it was the time of the morning that if I used the radio, any of my bosses coming to work would hear me. I also knew that I could not leave my neighbor with the deer and just drive off. I made the decision to use the police radio and call for assistance. My call number that I used when driving a police vehicle was 1161.

I got on the police radio and stated my call number. I told the dispatcher that I had received information that someone had struck a deer and I gave the location. As if things were not bad enough, the dispatcher asked for my call number again. He then asked me what my location was and I told him. By this time, I figured, shit, I'm already in trouble I might as well go all the way. I repeated my location and asked the dispatcher to notify Baltimore County police to have a car respond to the location.

The county officer arrived and was inquiring why I was out in the county with a Baltimore City police car. I actually told him the story, not that it mattered to him. He went over and looked at the deer. He said that he had received calls in the past for deer that had been struck by vehicles on this particular road. He went to the trunk of his car and retrieved a shot gun.

Being a city cop, I was awestruck by how casual he was about shooting this deer. I assumed by his actions that he had done this before. He walked toward the deer. He said I want to make sure I kill him with one shot. Even though I was a homicide detective and had seen a lot of bloody scenes, I didn't want to look when the shot was fired. The officer stood about three feet from the deer and fired one shot.

The officer took my neighbor's name and asked him if his vehicle was drivable. My neighbor said he was fine and drove off down Falls Road. I was getting in my car when the officer came over and asked for my name and address. I asked what he would do with the deer. I'm not sure if he was kidding or not, but he said he was taking the deer up the road to a volunteer fire station and gut it. I acted if that was normal...not being a hunter, I didn't know if you could do that after the deer had been hit by a car and shot. Whatever he was going to do, I didn't really give a shit, I just wanted to get to work.

I got to work a little late, but no one questioned me about why I was late. The day went as usual in the Homicide Unit. My partner and I went out to try to find some witnesses on a murder we were working on. I did tell my partner about my neighbor hitting a deer and the county police coming to the scene. I told him that I had to use my call number and just hoped that none of the bosses heard me calling in from a location in Baltimore County.

We got off work at a normal time that day. Most days in the Homicide Unit meant that you worked overtime trying to solve the many murders that plagued Baltimore City. My partner and a few others from the unit went to our favorite watering hole, the Calvert House. We always justified our going to have a few drinks…was to beat the traffic. There were many nights that we beat the hell out of traffic…because there is very little traffic when we left the bar at midnight.

We were drinking and talking about what we did that day or how we were doing on clearing prior murders. We were also talking about what men talk about in a bar: women, sports, politics, women, the weather, women, and that's about it…did I mention women.

About 7 P.M. our boss, the captain of the Homicide Unit, came in the bar. He was not a regular at the Calvert House but did stop in on occasion. He was a hell of a nice guy and probably the best captain they ever had in the Homicide Unit. I have written about him in my first book.

We were all talking and having a good time. The captain, Jim Cadden, came over to me and asked if he could talk to me. We moved to the side of the bar and out of hearing range of the others. He started with small talk; *how you doing, how's work, how's your family,* and then it got interesting. He said, "Richard, where are you living these days?"

I didn't think that question was out of the ordinary until the next question came. "Richard, what call number do you use in our unit?"

Now it's starting to really get interesting…I found myself going on the defensive as I felt something coming.

"Captain, I use call number 1161."

The captain was standing there just shaking his head when I responded to his questions. I was starting to feel those familiar little sweat beads forming on my neck and back. I guess the captain picked up on it when I started running my fingers under my shirt collar trying to get some sweat bead relief.

The captain paused and sipped his cosmopolitan. I never did know what the hell was in a cosmopolitan drink. We all got a kick out of him when he would walk in a bar and order a cosmopolitan. I have never been in the company of anyone that ordered a cosmopolitan. I now know what goes into that drink; vodka, orange liqueur, cranberry juice, triple sec, and lime juice. I'll stick with my gin and tonic.

I knew what was coming next and it did. "Richard, did you call on a police radio this morning that a deer had been struck?"

I had already had three drinks and was feeling pretty good. Before the captain could continue his barrage of questions, I decided to play the humble card. I first asked him if he wanted another cosmopolitan and he declined. Captain Cadden had been around a long time and was not the guy you wanted to try to bullshit.

"Captain, I know where you're going with the questioning. I did call in this morning because my neighbor hit a deer on his way to work. I was behind him in a police car. I had no choice but to stop and help the guy. I took the car home last night because I worked late. I knew I had to be back in the office in the morning."

The captain smiled as if he had just broken a murder case. "Richard, I think I'll take you up on that drink now."

I ordered the cosmo and thought that the drink would go in my favor...I was wrong.

"Richard, if you had told me the truth right off the bat, I would probably let this slide. You decided to beat around the bush and play me for a fool. I'm not used to my detectives pulling shit like this on me. You know, sometimes when you fuck up, it's best to take your licking like a man. If I am so inclined, I could charge you with using a police vehicle for personal reasons."

At this point, I could do nothing but stand there and hope that the second cosmo loosened him up a little. I was in no position to try to say anything. I figured the worse that could come out of this would be to lose my police permit to drive a vehicle. I knew it was not a violation that would require him charging me with anything serious. He could transfer me out of the Homicide Unit.

He actually walked away from me and started talking to some guys at the bar. I didn't know whether to stand where I was or try to pony up to the bar and hope that it was over. I stood down the end of the bar, always looking to see if he was coming back for more tongue lashing.

A short time later, I heard the captain telling some guys that he was going home. He walked toward me. I was going to say I was sorry for what I did. I looked at him and before I could say anything, he said, "Richard, I'll see you tomorrow. Don't drink too much the rest of the night."

I told him I appreciated him not charging me with any departmental rule violations. I reached out to shake his hand. He hesitated for a second but did shake hands. He started to walk away and turned back abruptly, "Richard, if you ever lie to me again, you'll find your ass walking a foot post on the midnight shift around the Greenmount Cemetery. I hope you will take this as a lesson learned...have a good night."

Before my bar buddies could come over and ask me what happened, I motioned for Crystal, the barmaid. How come most barmaids are named Crystal? I was shaking off the sweat beads and feeling a little better.

"Crystal, give me one of those cosmopolitans. I don't give a damn what's in it. I know when it's time to change. If it's good enough for the captain, then bring it on. The captain and I are cosmos guys from here on out."

Conversation # 13

In these next few conversations, I'm going to talk about some situations that I've had over the years with police cars.

I told you in the last conversation a story about taking a car home when I was not supposed to. I had also previously told you about backing a police car over a hill, almost dropping the car onto the highway below. I told you about running over a robbery suspect with a police car. Well, the car stories I'm going to tell you now are just as crazy.

First crazy police car story: When I left the Homicide Unit to work in the Arson Unit, I had a take home unmarked police car. The car had all the bells and whistles on it. The car had a police radio, a fire department radio, a siren, a loud speaker system, and best of all, it provided me free parking in the police garage. I was the only sergeant in the detective unit that had a take home car. The reason for the take home car was for me to respond to fatal fires and multi-alarm fires when called by the fire department.

In the Arson Unit, we also had an on-call detective who responded whenever the fire department needed him. The car I had was a real benefit to me as you can imagine. I never had to purchase gas, I parked in the police building, and I had no restrictions on where I could drive the car.

After work sometimes...actually lots of times, we would stop for a beer...actually several beers, we would stay about an hour...actually several hours, and that's where this conversation starts.

I stopped down the Inner Harbor at Phillips Restaurant with a couple detectives. I decided to park the unmarked police car on the promenade close to the restaurant. I knew this was not the best thing to do, but it was cold and I could see the car from the bar. I knew that if a uniform officer working the area came by, he would see the radios in the car and know it was a police car.

As usual, I stayed in the bar a little too long and stopped looking out the window for the car. About three hours after parking the car, I decided to leave the bar and go somewhere else.

I walked out and it was dark outside. I looked for the car and it was not where I parked it. I walked around thinking maybe I parked it someplace else.

I knew exactly where I parked it and walking around was stupid. I was getting worried. I saw a uniform cop walking by and I asked him if he had seen my car. I described the car and he said he did not see it. Now, I'm getting freaked out. Did someone actually steal an unmarked police car parked illegally in the Inner Harbor?

The guys that I had been drinking with had already left the bar. I went back in the bar and asked around if anyone had seen a green Ford LTD parked outside. It was interesting. Everyone I talked to told me that it was illegal to park a car there...I already knew that. After asking several people, I stopped; it was embarrassing to tell them that I was a police officer, the car was mine, and I can't find it.

I had the thought of calling for a uniform car to take a stolen car report. I nixed that thought really quick. I can imagine what the report would say...*an off-duty police sergeant parked his unmarked vehicle in an illegal parking space...went into the bar, stayed there for several hours drinking, came out to drive home while intoxicated, but the car was not there.*

If that report would ever get written, I could attach my badge, gun, and ID card to the report and get right in the unemployment line.

I decided to walk back to the police headquarters building, which was not that far. When I got there, I used a phone in the lobby to call the city impound lot. If the vehicle had been towed, it would be at that lot. It was a little embarrassing asking the lot attendant if there was a green Ford LTD on their lot. I had to tell him it was an unmarked police car and the questions started. I asked him to please not ask so many questions. Is the car on the lot or not? He checked all incoming vehicles and they did not have the car.

I still did not want to report it stolen. My next bright idea was to simply check out another car from the motor pool. I went to the motor pool office and checked out a vehicle. I'm not sure what the hell the plan was, but I figured I would just go home. If you're thinking this is the craziest thing you have ever heard, you're right. That's what a couple of drinks...actually more than a couple drinks will do to your thought process.

I was walking up the ramp of the parking section of the headquarters building to look for the car that I checked out. As I turned on the second level, I almost shit myself...literally, there was my green Ford LTD parked in a spot. I leaned against the wall for several minutes. Did I really park this car in the Inner Harbor? Did I walk to the Inner Harbor and never had the car? Is this a sick fuckin joke somebody is playing on me?

I cautiously walked to the driver side. I noticed a sheet of paper on the windshield. I stared at it for a few minutes, afraid to touch it. Did I need the crime lab to process it? Was somebody watching me when I read it? How did the car get back in the parking lot? I had the keys. Before I looked at the paper, I used my keys to open the door. I looked around the inside and nothing was missing. I pulled the paper from under the wipers. It read as follows:

Sarge, hope we didn't cause you any problems. We were down the harbor and saw your car. We decided to play a prank on you. You're always pulling shit on us, so we decided we would get you back. We got the spare keys from the motor pool. Have a nice night...

Holy shit...if I knew who did this, I would go right to their house and shoot the bastard. I read the note again, trying to identify the printing. How the fuck do you identify printing? Maybe the next morning at work, I could have all the detectives print this message. I got in the car and after shaking for several minutes, I started the car and went home.

The next morning, I drove to work and parked the car in my assigned spot in the building. I had the note from the night before in my briefcase. My plan was to just walk in the office, say good morning to the detectives, grab a cup of coffee, and sit at my desk.

The Arson Unit office was set up like a classroom. My desk sat at the far end as you entered. The six detectives in the unit had their desk facing mine, three on each side of the office. I'm not sure why we set it up this way, but it seemed like a good idea at the time. The routine would be that we would all be at our desk until roll call, which would be held down the hallway.

I sat at my desk pretending to read some reports. I was actually peering over the report and watching reactions from the detectives. I knew that one or maybe two of these guys pulled the prank on me last night. I didn't notice anything unusual, but these guys were good at pranks; I knew it would be hard to find the culprit.

Before roll call, I grabbed one of the guys in the hallway. I figured I would take my chances with the one in the unit who really didn't like pranks. I asked if he had heard anything in the office before I got in. I went a little further and told him what happened with the car. I hit the jackpot. Before we got to the roll call room, I had the name and the whole story.

Our roll call was very informal. We all just sat around while the lieutenant read out material that came down from the higher echelon. Now, I knew who my target was...I'm feeling pretty good. As roll call went on, I stared at the culprit. I knew I was on the right track, because I could see him with a smirk on his face. The smirk went to a smile, then a silly giggle, to a covering of the face, to a guilty laughter...I had my man.

After roll call, the detectives would let me know what they were working on and where they were going. My culprit told me he was going out to interview some witnesses on an arson. I asked him to stay back, that I wanted to talk to him about something. He sat at his desk fumbling with some papers. I told him I would be right back. I wanted him to experience the little sweat beads on his back that I had experienced the night before. I made sure I would let him sit and stew for a while.

I went and talked to the lieutenant about some investigations. I went back in my office about fifteen minutes later and he was still fumbling with papers. I shut the door and went to my desk. I sat there and just stared at him. I could see he was getting very uncomfortable. Finally, I went and sat next to his desk. He backed up a little and had a shit-eating-grin on his face. I asked him what was so funny. He said, "You have been staring at me all morning. Now, you ask me to hang back. What's up, what did I do?"

Now I was smiling, "Who said you did anything? I just want to have a little talk with you. Do you know what kind of unmarked car I drive?"

"Yeah, you drive a green Ford LTD, why do you ask?"

I was kind of feeling sorry for him at this point. He knew I had him. With just him and I in the room, he was feeling the pinch. I figured I had messed with him long enough. I had played a lot of pranks on people and had been caught many times. I knew what he was going through.

"Were you down the Inner Harbor last night by any chance?"

He squirmed, turned away a little and said, "Okay, who the fuck told you what I did?"

Now I was the one with the smile on my face. I told him, "I would not want to hold up a bank with you. You gave it up before I even got into the tough questions. I knew it was you from the minute I walked in the office this morning. You had the biggest guilty look on your face. Nobody told me that you took my car and moved it back to the motor pool. You know, I really ain't mad at you. It was a well thought out prank; who else was involved in this with you?"

I decided to let him off the hook. I never pursued who else was involved. I had my bad guy and that was enough satisfaction for me. It was time to move on.

I do remember thinking all that day about, *what the hell can I do to this guy that would come close to what he did to me.*

We all know that paybacks are bitch...I love paybacks.

I know that in my twenty-five years with the police department, I have either participated in or been the victim of some really thought out pranks. If I put all the pranks on paper, I could write another book............ *Nah.*

Conversation #14

<u>Next crazy police car story:</u>

When I started in the Arson Unit, I knew very little about fire investigation. I was fortunate enough to hook up with a few outstanding fire department investigators. These guys had on average, twenty-five years of fire investigation experience. They were all captains and they were assigned to the Baltimore Fire Department, Fire Investigation Bureau. We worked very close with these men. They would respond to the fire scene and determine how the fire started. We in the Arson Unit would take over the investigation if it was determined to be a set fire.

Not having any fire investigation experience, my lieutenant decided to send me to Philadelphia to attend a week-long fire investigation school. I drove to Philly in my assigned unmarked police car. This was not the Ford LTD in the previous conversation. The car in this story was a 1979 Ford Fairlane.

The school was conducted at a police facility just outside of Philadelphia. There were forty law enforcement officers attending the school. Some of the attendees were local and some were from cities on the East Coast. Most of the attendees drove to the school in unmarked police vehicles.

We stayed at a Holiday Inn which was about twenty minutes from where the training was to be held. On the first day, we basically just met each other and received information on the curriculum for the training. One of the local police officers who was also a member of the training staff, talked to us about where to eat, where to go in Philly, and also where not to go.

After class on the first day we went back to the Holiday Inn and had a drink at the bar. We talked about where we would go for dinner in the area. My travel to the school, my lodging, and my meals were all covered by my police agency. The per diem for the day was not that much, so the choices of where to eat were limited. About ten of us decided on a restaurant close to the hotel.

It didn't take long for us to make acquaintances. When cops get together, the theme is always the same…stories about where you work. I quickly made friends with two cops from Philly, one from New Jersey, and one from New York. I think we clicked because of where we were sitting at the table.

After dinner, we went back to the hotel and sat in the lobby continuing to tell stories about our particular police agencies. A guy from Philly who had a name you can't forget, Tony Pantaloni, asked us if we wanted to go to a nightclub later in the evening. Tony made it known early on that he wanted to be called *Pants*; that's what his fellow officers on the Philly PD called him. Pants said the nightclub was close by. He said it was a hotspot for the area we were in. Most of us agreed and decided to meet later in the lobby to drive to the nightclub.

We met in the lobby at about 8 P.M. We broke up in groups of four and headed out to the club...we took three cars. I drove my unmarked car with Pants and two other guys in the car. Pants was in the front seat with me. I asked him about the club we were going to. He said it was called, *The Big Bear.* He said the club had live music every night.

We got to the club and sure enough it had a big bear on top of the building. After parking the cars, we went in after we paid a small cover charge. The place was huge and the band had already started playing. We found a spot on the far side of the club where we could see the very large dance floor. We commenced to drink. It wasn't long before the club was filling up. I was surprised that on a Monday night the crowd would be so packed. The bartender said the club is filled every night except Sunday when they are closed.

As the night went on, we were knocking down the drinks pretty good. I think we had a tab going, but I don't remember what the final toll was. I actually don't remember a whole lot about the later part of the night. I was told the next day that we closed the club up at 1 A.M.

The training was to start in the morning, which would have been Tuesday. The plan was to drive to the training location in our vehicles. Those who did not have a vehicle would hook up with someone that had a vehicle. The classes were to start at 8 A.M.

I can tell you now that I did not even remember going back to the hotel that night or early morning. When I woke up I had the worse headache imaginable. I made my way to the bathroom to take a shower and shave. When I came out of the bathroom, I saw the clock on the dresser…it was 9:15 A.M. I'm thinking…*holy shit I missed the first day of training.*

As I was struggling with the headache, I tried to find the phone number for the school. Not sure what I would tell them, but I would come up with something. I found the number and called the school. I told a secretary to tell the instructor that I was sick, but I would make it to the training as soon as possible. I fumbled around finding the clothes I would wear which were still in my suitcase.

I got dressed and went down to the lobby. I grabbed a coffee and a doughnut from the small eating area. I ran out to the parking lot. I looked around for my car. The lot was quite full. I went up and down each aisle but could not find my car. I went back inside and told the desk clerk that I could not find my car. He went out to the parking lot and we both went over the entire lot, but no car in sight.

We went back in and I told the clerk that I guess my car had been stolen. He said he had been working for the hotel for several years and they had never had a car stolen off the lot. I was arguing with him that there is always a first for everything and this must be it.

After my insisting that the car was stolen, he said he would call the Pennsylvania State Police. He must have told them that my car was a police car because they were there within minutes. The trooper that came in the hotel could have been the poster boy for the Pennsylvania State Police. He looked very sharp in his trooper outfit. He was about six feet four and probably weighed well over two hundred pounds. He introduced himself. I told him who I was and what training I was attending. He was familiar with the location of the training. He told me the same thing the clerk had told me; there had not been any cars stolen off this parking lot in several years. He asked me to go out and show him where I parked the car. I went out with him, but I had no idea where in the hell I parked the car. He asked me to sit in his car while he took a report. We were just getting into the report when he said, "By the way, did you guys go out last night and did you take your car?"

"Yes, we did go out last night, but what does that have to do with my car being stolen?"

I knew where he was going with these questions. I started to think while he was writing...*I don't even remember coming back to the hotel, much less actually driving my car.* He stopped writing, "Where did you guys go last night, do you remember?"

How can you forget a name like *The Big Bear*?

"Yes, I do remember where we went...the place was called *The Big Bear.*"

I no sooner got the words out of my mouth, when he said, "Why didn't you tell me that earlier? Are you sure you drove your car back to the hotel when you left the bar?"

I tried to play it like I was offended by the question. "I'm sure I drove the car back. How else would I have gotten back to the hotel?"

The trooper put his writing materials away and told me to buckle up. I asked why should I buckle up if we are parked...seemed like a reasonable question coming from a guy still suffering from a hangover and a terrific headache. I buckled up and he said, "Just for the hell of it, let's take a ride up to *The Big Bear.* It's only a few miles up the road."

I didn't answer, but while he was driving, I'm thinking what if the car is still on the lot of *The Big Bear*. Would the guys I was with last night do that to me? Would they allow me to leave my car there? It felt like more than a few miles up the road. The trooper was quiet during the ride. I wanted to say something but could not find the exact words. If the car is on the lot, I'm going to feel like a complete asshole to this fellow law enforcement officer.

We pulled into the empty lot...that is the empty lot except for my car sitting there all by itself. Before we pulled close to my car, the trooper asked if that was my car. I put on a really bad act as if I was surprised that the car was there.

"Well, I'll be damned, what do you know, it's my car all right."

As we pulled close to the car, I could see that the driver's side door was open. Now I'm feeling really embarrassed as the trooper is snickering, trying like hell to not just bust out laughing. We got out of the trooper's car and looked my car over. Other than the door being opened all night, there was no damage. The trooper asked if I had the key. I said, sure I have the key. I began the humbling search for the keys. I went in every pocket. I was almost ready to say, someone must have stolen the keys…but I caught myself because this very nice trooper seemed like he was getting less amused at all of this. I did not have the keys. I told the trooper that they were probably back at the hotel. He took a step back and gave me a weird Pennsylvania State Police Trooper look. I knew from the look that he pretty much had enough with me. I asked if he could take me back to get the key…mistake. He folded his arms up to his chest and said, "Let's do this, I'll take you to the school that you're supposed to be at. I can get you there is twenty minutes. You can tell them any story you want. After your training, one of your buddies can bring you back to your car. We can lock the car. Make sure whoever brings you back has cables to jump start the car."

I had no choice but to agree with him and get my ass to that training. The ride to the school with the trooper seemed like it would go on forever. Occasionally, he would look over at me and shake his head. He had the look like he wanted to just bust out laughing. I tried some small talk about things like: how long have you been a trooper, do you live in the area you patrol, do you like your job? His answers were one-liners and he appeared to be bored with the questions. I guess I should have asked him if he had ever had a stupid out of town cop lose his police car at the *Big Bear* before.

We arrived at the school and he actually became a little friendlier. He shook my hand and said, "Listen dude, I know what happens when cops get together for a few drinks. I've been in your shoes on a few occasions. Although, I can say that I have never been that dumb that I didn't know where I left my car. You better get in your school. As far as my call to the hotel for a stolen car, I'll just write it up as a man seeking some advice."

I thanked him and apologized for wasting his time. I went in the building and was directed to the classroom where the training was being held. I opened the door and instantly all eyes were directed right at me. I looked for an empty seat…in the rear of the room. The class had just returned from a break. As the guys were taking their seats, they were looking at me and trying not to laugh. I was motioning to the guys that were with me at the *Big Bear*. I was mouthing to them…*what the hell happened last night*?

I wanted to holler out...*why the fuck didn't you assholes take care of me and how in the hell did I get back to the hotel?*

I decided to just take my seat. I no sooner sat down when the instructor said, "Sergeant Ellwood, welcome to our class that started at eight o'clock. We missed you and were really concerned about you. Some of the guys told me about what happened last night at the *Big Bear*. We talked about it for quite a while this morning...it's very amusing. Is there anything you can add to the story that we don't already know?"

I just sat there and took it all in. I really had no response to what he said. I did notice that while he was talking, he was smiling, so I knew he was screwing with me. The guys that were at the *Big Bear* with me just looked at me and were shaking their heads as if they could not believe I was still alive.

The instructor walked down the aisle toward me and shook my hand. I was not expecting that and was waiting for what was coming next. He addressed the class and said, "Gentlemen, Sergeant Ellwood has become a victim of the *Big Bear*. He is not the first cop who attended this school that has fallen prey to the big claws of the *Big Bear*. We always seem to have one attendee that doesn't show up on time the first day of school. Don't worry about anything Sergeant Ellwood, you are amongst friends and fellow police officers. On behalf of the guys that were with you at the Big Bear...they all have one question and one comment...

Do you remember who you left the Big Bear with last night? If you do remember, then the comment is...you better get some fucking stronger glasses...now let's start our training."

Conversation # 15

This conversation could be described as...*What goes around, comes around.*

In 1978, after thirteen years on the police department, I got promoted to sergeant. I was working in the Homicide Unit at the time. When the assignments for the newly promoted sergeants came out, I was surprised that I was being assigned to the Tactical Unit.

It was interesting how they made the assignments. A friend who was working in the Burglary Unit and also getting promoted, was being assigned to the Homicide Unit. This did not make much sense. I was already in the Homicide Unit; why not just keep me there. I questioned it but was told that the captain of the Tactical Unit had made a special request to get me in his unit. The captain was a former Marine and we had worked together when he was my sergeant. I guess he figured that me being a Marine also was reason enough to get me in his unit.

In the Tactical Unit, I was a sergeant in the QRT (Quick Response Team) or more commonly referred to in most departments as SWAT (Small Weapons Assault Team). I enjoyed my time in the Tactical Unit and have written about it in my first book.

The story I want to convey in this book, has nothing to do with the work we did in the Tactical Unit. I must first take you back many years when I was working a patrol car with Joe Bolesta. The year was 1968 and we were working a two-man car. We heard a call come over the police radio for a burglary in progress at Jack's restaurant in the 1100 block Lombard Street. Jack's was a corned beef sandwich shop and had been in business since 1965. The store was owned by Jack Goldenson.

When we arrived at the store, we went around back. Just as we pulled the police car in the rear, we observed a man coming out of a window of the store. We apprehended him and he was subsequently charged with breaking into the store. He had taken cash from some of the registers. It was procedure in those days to have the owner come to the store and check and see what was taken.

Jack Goldenson came to his store and was very appreciative of us catching the guy who broke into the store. He told us that in the future, if we were in the area of his store, to stop in and get a sandwich.

Well, being the good cops that we were and having great memories, we decided to take Jack up on his offer. A few weeks later we went in the store. We walked through the line and we each got a corned beef sandwich, potato chips, and a soda. We saw Jack at one of the cash registers and got in line. When we placed the food and drinks on the counter, he rang it up. He appeared to not even recognize us as the two cops who caught the burglar. Without even looking at us, he said, "That will be four dollars and fifty cents."

Not sure if that was the exact amount, but you get the point. We both just stood there looking at Jack. I was about to pull some money out to pay for the stuff. Before I could do it, Joe said, "You don't even remember us, do you?"

Jack looked us over and said, "Are you the cops who caught the guy who broke into my place?"

Joe told him that we were…and now we're thinking that we are getting the food and drink for free. Jack said that he really appreciated us catching the guy. Well, I'm not sure how much he really appreciated it because he then said, "Gentlemen, just give me three dollars. I'll give you a break for the good work you did."

Well, I could see the blood rushing to Joe's face. Joe was a fairly new cop at the time, but he was very street smart. Knowing him back then, you would have thought he had a lot of time on the job. He was also a very imposing guy at six four and about two hundred pounds. Joe leaned over toward Jack and said, "Mr. Jack, you mean to tell me that you're charging us for these sandwiches after we caught a guy that broke into this place? Are you the same guy who told us to stop in when we were in the area? Well, Mr. Jack I was going to tell you to shove these sandwiches up your ass, but instead, we will pay you the four dollars and fifty cents."

Jack just stood there. He didn't know what to say. I know one thing he didn't say and that was *I'll give you the sandwiches*. We paid him and walked out. I think when we were almost at the door, he hollered to us that he was sorry.

We went and parked somewhere and ate the food. We were furious that he would not even consider giving us the damn sandwiches. I remember Joe saying that if he ever had the opportunity in the future to get back at Jack he would do it.

Well, now we can fast forward to 1978. I'm a newly promoted uniform sergeant working patrol in the area of Jack's. I was hungry and decided to go in Jack's for a corned beef sandwich. As I entered the place, it hit me like a ton of bricks. The memory of that day back in 1968 came to light. I saw Jack, but I knew he would not remember me from that incident.

I was walking toward the counter to order a sandwich when Jack hollered to me, "Officer, come over here!"

At first, I thought he might have recognized me and wanted to congratulate me on my promotion, but that was not the case. He had no idea who I was. When I walked over to him, he was talking very loud and waving his hands. He was motioning toward the bathroom and shouting. I asked him to calm down and tell me what the problem was. He said, "Sarge, I want you to go in the men's room and arrest the "bum" that is eating my sandwich."

I didn't quite grasp what the hell he was saying. I asked him again what he was talking about. He said that a bum (that was his words, not mine) came in the store, walked through the line, picked up a corned beef sandwich, and went in the bathroom. Jack said he looked in and saw the man eating the sandwich while sitting on the floor. Jack kept saying to me that he wanted the bum arrested.

His excitement was causing a lunch time crowd to gather around to see what was happening. I told Jack that I would check it out. I went in the men's room and sure enough, the man (a homeless man) was sitting on the floor. The wrapper from the sandwich was next to him. He still had some mustard on his face from the sandwich. At first the man appeared to be scared of me. I knelt down next to him and asked him what he was doing. He said that he was homeless and hungry. He admitted that he came in the store and picked up a sandwich and ate it. It was hard to determine, but the man appeared to be in his fifties. He did not appear to have been drinking and that would not have put him in the class that Jack put him in as a bum.

I helped him to his feet. He kept telling me he was sorry and just wanted to get back out on the street. I'm not sure why, but I was feeling sorry for this man.

What in life put him in this predicament that left him looking very old and obviously homeless? When he was on his feet, I first thought about just paying for his sandwich. Then my memory of years gone by clicked in. I told the man to wipe the mustard off his face and straighten himself up as much as he could. I told him that when we walked out of the bathroom, to just keep walking out of the store. He gave me a weird look as if he didn't believe me. I assured him that he was not being arrested for eating the sandwich.

We walked out of the bathroom together and the homeless man kept on walking to the door. Jack was standing there and started to yell, "Officer, I told you I wanted him arrested."

I told Jack, "First of all Mr. Jack, I'm a sergeant, not an officer. It took me thirteen years to make sergeant, please give me some respect. As far as arresting that man for eating a sandwich, I can't do that. I did not see the man eat the sandwich. When I went in the bathroom, I only saw him sitting on the floor. If you want to have him arrested, you will have to go to the station and fill out some paperwork. You will then have to apply for an arrest warrant. If you want to do all that, I'll get his name for you."

Jack was extremely upset to say the least. He told me that he would be calling my supervisor. I told him that I was the supervisor. I told him that if he had a complaint, he should call the station in the morning and talk to my captain. He proceeded to tell me how he took care of all the police officers who come into his restaurant.

I turned to leave and had the greatest impulse to turn and tell him...*he sure as shit didn't take care of two cops years ago who caught a burglar breaking into his joint.*

I left the store and when I got to my car, I sat there with a big grin on my face. I was thinking of my former partner, Joe Bolesta. I wish he was still around. He passed away a few years ago before the writing of this book. I know he would have been proud of me for letting the homeless man go; even if my motive was not so much as to help a homeless man. He was just the means available to let me and Joe get back at Jack for being a cheap bastard. Knowing Joe, he would have got the biggest kick out of me telling everyone this story.

Life is funny, you never know when you will have such an opportunity to get back at someone.

I guess I won't be eating at Jack's in the future.

Conversation # 16

I think it's time to have a conversation about a period of time in the police department that I considered some of the best and most exciting days on the job. I'm talking about my years working in the Vice Unit.

I was fortunate enough to have worked in both the Central District Vice Unit and the Northeast District Vice Unit. Looking back on those times, it was very unusual for someone to work in a vice unit in two different districts. It was also customary in those days to work in a vice unit for no more than about three years. Having worked in two different vice units for a total of five years was probably because I could write a mean search warrant...*nothing but the truth, so help me God.*

In the Central District Vice Unit, I worked for Sergeant Pete Bailey. I have written about Pete in this book and my first book...*Cop Stories-The Few, The Proud, The Ugly.* We had a great time. You could not work for a better person than Pete Bailey. My partner was Joe Bolesta, who I have talked about a lot in this book. I also write about Joe in my first book. I'm sure he is looking down on me and telling me to let everyone know about the great times we had working together.

Let's start with all three of us...Pete, Joe, and me having a drinking contest on *The Block* one night. For those that are not local in Baltimore, *The Block* was an adult entertainment section of the city. It was known for strip joints which were located in downtown Baltimore. It was actually a tourist attraction for men when they came to town on business or conventions.

We worked eight at night to four in the morning because that was when the vice action was at its peak. Sometimes we would just relax late at night, especially if we made an arrest earlier. On one of these relaxing nights, we decided that we would frequent some joints on *The Block*. We were kidding about having one drink at each place. I have to admit, that although we were cops in plainclothes, every club on *The Block* knew who we were.

We started at about eleven at night. We didn't get very far when we stopped in the Gay White Way. The place was owned by a guy named, Nicky Orfice. Nicky loved when we stopped in to have a drink. On this night things got a little carried away. Nick was in the mood to drink. He challenged us to a whiskey drinking contest. Nick drank only the best and at that time, Crown Royal was the best.

Nick told his bartender to put a bottle of Crown Royal on the bar. He got four shot glasses. I'll cut to the chase on this story. I bailed out of the contest at two shots. I was not then, and never have been a whiskey drinker. On the other hand, Pete and Joe were frequent flyers on drinking shots of whiskey. I think Joe got up to seven shots and Nick stopped at eight. Pete was at seven and just to win, he drank two more. He drank a total of nine shots...very competitive guy. He slammed his shot glass on the bar and declared himself the winner.

We stood around talking to Nick for a while, until we realized Pete was gone. We thought he was in the men's room, but he had left the club. Joe and I decided to check outside to see if he was sick. When we went outside, we saw the owner of the Ritz Club, a guy we knew as Kingie. He was a club owner that we were very friendly with. His club was directly across from The Gay White Way. He hollered for us to come over. When we got there, he said, "You got to get in my club. Your boss is up on the stage dancing!"

I was thinking, *holy shit, the sergeant in charge of the vice unit is up on the stage dancing...this ain't good.*

We went in the club and sure as shit, Pete was on the stage dancing. It appeared that the customers thought he was part of an act. Kingie closed and locked the front door so that no one else would come in. It was very clear to us that Pete was out of control from the nine shots of whiskey. We knew we had to get him off that stage. Pete was a stocky guy and very strong. I had seen him in some fights and he could handle himself pretty good. Joe was a big guy, I was not. We had to take our shot of getting him off the stage or bad things were going to happen.

We solicited the help of the bouncer, a guy name Jack. Before we went on the stage, Kingie asked the customers to leave. On the stage with Pete, were a couple of go-go girls and they were egging Pete on. The three of us went up on the stage. We tried to talk Pete into coming off. He refused and kept on dancing...to no music.

As Joe and Jack were the bigger guys, they decided that we would tackle Pete. Well, it was a task just to get him to the ground. He wasn't really trying to hurt anyone. He was just wailing around and hard to handle.

We finally got him to the floor. We were sitting on Pete to get him to calm down. Every once in a while, he would start to struggle again. We had to get him out of the club, but where would we take him?

Joe decided that we would get the car and just take him home. When we told him what we were going to do, he started to struggle again. This part sounds crazy, but we decided to tie him up with rope. You have to use your imagination on this. Here we were, two cops working in the vice unit, trying to get our sergeant who is tied up with rope into a car so we can deliver him home. Are you still with me on this?

The best part of this story is that we drove him home, still tied up. We knew Pete's wife and it would not be pretty when she sees him coming home drunk and tied up. When we got to the house, it appeared that he was falling asleep. We thought we could get him up the front steps and into the house without him waking up…mistake. We were lifting him out of the car when he woke up. He started struggling and screaming. We told him he was home. We knew his wife was going to kick his ass when she saw him. We took the rope off his legs as he appeared to be cooperating. We kept the rope on around his waist and hands.

When we rang the doorbell, he started to act up again. The door opened and the look on his wife's face was not good. She asked what happened and we tried to play it down a little. How in the hell can you play it down when two guys bring your husband home tied up with rope?

We stayed for a while and told her some story about Pete had a couple of drinks and got sick. We asked her if she wanted us to take the rope off. She said, "You guys can just leave…I'll take care of this." We left the house wondering what the hell was she going to do with Pete.

The next night at about eight o'clock, Pete walked into the vice office. Joe and I pretended we were busy. We tried to avoid eye contact with him. It was all we could do to keep from busting out laughing. We knew it was just a matter of time before he was going to ask what happened last night.

After several minutes of complete silence, Pete said, "Okay, knock off the bullshit. Stop with the silent treatment. What the hell happened last night?"

Before we could say anything, all three of us just busted out laughing. Finally, when the laughing stopped, I commenced to tell Pete what had happened. It was as if he was hearing it for the first time. Each time I would say something that sounded outrageous, he just shook his head. I could tell that he was getting embarrassed. He was feeling bad about what happened. It was not so much for himself, but for all the people that were involved in the foolishness the night before. At one point, he said, "Just stop, I think I have heard enough to get the picture. Why in the hell didn't you two assholes stop me?"

That's when we all commenced to laugh very loud again. We told him that everything was fine with the owner of the Ritz club. We told him that we did try to stop him, but he was fighting us all the way. I wanted to ask him what happened with his wife when we left him. I thought I would let that slide for a while. I didn't see any visible scratches or wounds on him. I figured he survived whatever took place after we left his house.

We went on the street and drove around for a while. Periodically, he would ask another question about the incident. We assured him that everything was fine. He asked whose idea was it to have the whiskey drinking contest. We told him it was Nicky's idea. Then he asked what I thought was a strange question.

"Who won the contest?"

We told him that he won by a landslide. I also told him that in a contest like that, no one can be the winner. He smiled and said, "I could have died drinking that much whiskey. As a matter of fact, compared to what happened at my house last night, I would have been better off dead."

The only good that came out of this incident was that I got to take home several of the pretty velvet bags that the Crown Royal came in. My kids loved those bags. We had plenty of them.

Conversation # 17

While working in the Vice Unit, we had the occasion to meet some really interesting characters that worked in the strip joints on *The Block*. They knew we were cops and we knew they were the bad guys. We knew each other's boundaries. They were not violent; they were just bad guys making a living.

We had the occasion to have breakfast with the man who was known to be the brains behind the biggest gambling operation in Baltimore. His name was Julius Salisbury. He was known around town as the "Lord." When I say we had breakfast with him; don't get the wrong idea. We knew he was the kingpin of all gambling operations in Baltimore. He also owned a strip club on *The Block*.

The breakfast encounter occurred one morning when Pete, Joe and I were eating breakfast in a restaurant near *The Block*. Salisbury walked in. He came over and sat with us. We didn't invite him; he just did it on his own. He was a very friendly man and respected by most people who came in contact with him. I'm sure he had his nasty side. You don't operate the biggest gambling operation in a city by being a nice guy all the time.

Salisbury sat with us and ordered a coffee. He introduced himself. We already knew who he was. He knew we were cops. I don't remember the conversation, but it was mostly personal stuff. He asked how long each had been on the department. I remember the three of us felt a little uncomfortable talking with him. We knew that at the time, every law enforcement agency was probably working to knock off his gambling business. We talked for about fifteen minutes. He wished us well and left the restaurant.

A couple years later, Salisbury was indicted on federal charges. At his trial, he was found guilty of racketeering. Before sentencing in federal court, he was ordered to be confined to his condo by the judge. His condo was being guarded twenty-four hours a day by the FBI.

Well, what happened will probably go down in history as one of the biggest blunders by the FBI. Salisbury got out of the condo and has never been found as of the writing of this book. There were so many theories of what happened. Whatever happened may never be known, he just disappeared.

I have heard so many stories about his disappearance. Rumors have it that he paid off the agents guarding him. He disguised himself as a female and walked away from the condo. Another theory was that the government actually helped him to disappear after he gave information on other gambling operations in the city. He somehow got out and went to Israel. The best one is that he got a sex change and is living somewhere as a female. If I have my pick of what happened, I'm saying that there are a couple of really rich FBI agents living in luxury somewhere today.

There have been several books written about Julius Salisbury. If he is still alive today, he would be about a hundred years old. So, if he's still alive, he's either an old man or an old lady, but either way, he pulled off the one of the greatest disappearances ever.

Moving on to another Vice Unit story:

While working in vice we met a very interesting club manager on *The Block* named Joe. His last name is not important. He was a scary looking guy. He was from Chicago. After getting to know him and talking to Joe, we found out that he was forced out of Chicago by *The Mob*. He told us that he came up short on a debt that was due to *The Mob*. He subsequently paid a big penalty before he fled.

Joe had that gangster type of voice. For the most part, you could believe he was telling you the truth. The main reason he left Chicago was that there was a "hit" put on his life by the *Chicago Mob*. He was visited by *The Mob* guys one night. He was severely beaten and left to die. He described it to us in very graphic detail what *The Mob* did to him. He was in a club when he was visited by several *Mob* guys. Although Joe appeared to be a pretty tough guy, he apparently was no match for his *Mob* visitors. He said that when they came in the club, they ordered everyone to leave. He was then beaten almost to the point where he was passing out. When he thought they were finished, they dragged him across the floor and lifted up one end of a pool table. They placed him under the lifted end and dropped the table on his face. Joe said he doesn't remember that part of the beating. He was told about it later by the club owner. He spent three weeks in the hospital and endured twelve surgeries to reconstruct his face. When he was released from the hospital, he went through several months of therapy to learn how to talk. His jaw had been reconstructed and he lost most of his teeth in the incident.

Joe said that when he recovered, he left Chicago and went to live with some family in New Jersey.

When he was telling us the story, you could tell he was still suffering from that horrible beating. He obviously had mental and physical scars from the beating. Joe was not a youngster. He was about fifty years old when we met him. He had some great stories about *The Mob* in Chicago. The stories included how the Chicago PD was so corrupt. He even said that the unit in the police department that investigated cops was corrupt. He had personally paid off cops while he was involved in the illegal gambling rackets in Chicago.

I'm not sure why Joe confided in us to the point that he frequently told stories about *The Mob*. He also seemed to enjoy talking about the corrupt Chicago Police Department.

When he came to Baltimore, he had decided that *The Mob* life he had been living was over. Although he was working on *The Block*, and always around unsavory characters, he said it was nothing like Chicago.

This is the conversation I want to convey to you about Joe. We were talking to him one night and he asked if we wanted to go to a party. We liked Joe but going to a party with a club manager on *The Block* would not be very smart. The more Joe talked about the party, it sounded interesting. He told us that a lot of the club owners from *The Block* would be there.

We knew most of the club owners from just being on *The Block* most every night. We told Joe that we would think about it and get back to him. We saw him a few nights later and he was insisting that we go to the party. He said, "If you feel uncomfortable being there, you can just leave."

My partner and I thought about it. We decided...*what the hell, let's do it. It would probably be very interesting standing around and listening to a bunch of strip club owners.*

The party was held late on a Saturday night. It was held at Joe's apartment in downtown Baltimore. We were surprised at how many people were there. We knew most of the club owners, but a lot of the people were complete strangers. We kept to ourselves and just watched and listened. Joe was making the rounds and was hitting the booze pretty good. Here comes the good part...

We were talking to Joe and he was quite drunk. He said, "Fellows, I got something I want to run by you."

The way he was looking around and talking a little softer, we assumed it was going to be another Chicago *Mob* story...boy, were we wrong. In that Chicago accent, he kind of nudged us away from the crowd and said, "I've been doing some thinking. I really trust you guys. I'm planning a big robbery."

Well, you can imagine what we were thinking when he said that. I thought he was just messing with us and it was a joke. But the more we watched his actions, we could tell he was serious. Cocking his head back and forth, he said, "I could sure use your help pulling this off. It won't be easy, but it would be very worthwhile to us all."

At this point we knew he was dead serious. What the hell do we do? He's asking two cops to help him do a robbery...*holy shit.*

Instead of just walking out, we decided to hear his big robbery plans. I asked him what kind of robbery was he planning. Joe nudged us even further away from the partiers. "Gentlemen, I'm talking about the payroll at Fort Meade."

I almost dropped my drink. I looked at my partner, and I think we were too stunned to say anything. You have to understand, working in a vice unit you are literally working undercover. I knew we were good at what we did. We were now having a guy who knew we were cops, asking us to commit a robbery with him. For him to ask that, it took balls...big balls.

We knew about Fort Meade. It's a huge Army base just outside the limits of the city. We could only imagine that a payroll from that base would be very big. I'm not sure how and why Joe would know anything about the payroll at Fort Meade. He told us to think it over. Think it over...what the hell is there to think over...we're cops. We don't rob Army bases.

Well, we left the party after telling Joe that he was the craziest bastard we had ever met. He laughed and told us that he was just testing us. Really, just testing us about robbing one of the biggest Army bases in the nation. I told you before, this guy was a whack job. Apparently when they dropped the pool table on his face, they must have crushed most of his brain.

I'm sure at this point, you are thinking, why didn't we go along with him and see if he was really planning such a robbery. Well, you had to know this guy like we thought we did. No way in the world would this idiot be able to pull off a robbery of a candy store, much less an Army base.

Now, moving on to an even better story about Joe, the crazy guy from Chicago. We were on *The Block* one night and talking to him. We were talking about owning and carrying a weapon. Out of the clear blue sky, Joe said, "Do you guys know how I can register a machine gun?"

After almost swallowing my double wad of gum, I decided to play along with him. I asked if he really had a machine gun and he said that he did. He said he had brought the gun with him when he left Chicago. If you're thinking this is a bullshit story, think again. Joe was a guy that was in *The Mob* in Chicago and had probably been in a lot of nefarious shit. I think if you could sit down with this guy for a period of time over some drinks, you would hear some horror stories about what he did in the Chicago *Mob*. His years in *The Mob* would have been in the '50s and '60s when *The Mob* culture was very active in many cities in America.

We were not taking advantage of his obvious and reckless demeanor. We were just having fun with a crazy son of a bitch. When you're a cop, you need to have some levity and fun to do the job. I'm sure you have to agree we certainly did that.

Without even asking more about the machine gun, we told Joe that he could take the weapon to the Federal Building and get it registered. We told him to put it in a shopping bag and not carry it openly to the building...as if we really had to tell someone this. We laughed about it and had no more discussion with him about the machine gun.

A few days later we were down on *The Block*. The owner of the club where Joe worked saw us. He motioned for us to come in his place. When we went in, he asked us to go to his office. He wanted to tell us something. In his office, he closed the door and we were wondering what the hell could he want. After closing the door, he sat in his chair. He lit a cigar and said, "You ain't going to believe what happened to Joe."

Before he said anything more, we looked at each other and almost simultaneously we were probably thinking, *because it's Joe, it must be something really wild.*

He leaned forward in his chair. He blew some cigar smoke out the side of his mouth and said, "The stupid bastard took a machine gun up to the Federal Building today and asked to get it registered."

Well, I didn't have any more gum to swallow, but I came close to swallowing my tongue. Holy shit, the dumb bastard believed us. He took the gun to register it...you can't register a machine gun. We sat there and could not laugh; it would have been to obvious that we had something to do with it. The club owner asked if we could try to help him out. What the hell could we do? Could we go down to the Federal Building and say, *hey guys we told this dude to bring the machine gun in to register it?*

We were feeling bad for poor Joe. I asked the club owner what we could do. He shook his head and said, "I'm not sure what you could do. Joe has a fifty-thousand-dollar bail set on him. He's being held on the charge of possessing a machine gun. I called my lawyer and he told me that the only place you can register a machine gun is with the Secretary of State."

Well, don't feel too sorry for Joe. We later found out that the ATF got involved and the gun was not functional. He did appear before a federal judge. We were told later that he told the judge that a couple of friends told him to go to the Federal Building and register the machine gun. Apparently, the judge figured this guy was so stupid that trying to get a conviction in court would be a waste of time.

We did see Joe a couple of weeks later and he was not even mad at us. He actually laughed about the incident. We continued to be friends with Joe.

Many months after this incident, we were told that Joe went back to Chicago. I'm not sure why he went back. I bet he is telling his former *Mob* guys about two cops in Baltimore who would not do a robbery with him and they also sent him to the Federal Building to register his machine gun.

Joe was a great guy to listen to about all his Chicago *Mob* stories. He came up real short in the common-sense area. I guess it's a good thing that the bad guys aren't so smart or we would never catch them.

Conversation # 18

One more conversation I'll have with you about my time in the Vice Unit. It's a story that is talked about when my fellow retired cops and I get together.

One of the areas you work when you're in a Vice Unit is prostitution. I have talked about making arrest for prostitution in my first book. I think I might actually still hold the record for making the most arrest for prostitution in one night while working in the Vice Unit. I actually arrested thirteen prostitutes in a span of about three hours one hot summer night. I'm not going to go into the details in this book...it's all in my first book.

The story I want to talk about in this book involves making raids on houses of ill repute or more commonly known as whorehouses. The ladies that sold their wares for money, usually had a place to take the men. We would sometimes just follow the car after the prostitute got in. I have had occasions where I was solicited and went to a house with a prostitute. The arrest was made as soon as I entered the house. No exchange of money had to take place and certainly no jumping in bed with them. We do have some morals...not many, but we do have some.

When you were going to raid a location for prostitution you needed a search warrant to enter the property. In the warrant, you would have to lay out in much detail what you suspected in the house you wanted to enter. It was not that tough. We would just watch the house suspected of prostitution. We would list how many men we saw going in the house, how long they were there, who owned the location, the time of night or early morning hours, and any other pertinent information. We would take the warrant to a judge, get it signed, and watch the location for the right time to execute the warrant.

Serving a search warrant on any location could be very dangerous. With a warrant, you did not have to knock and wait for the door to open. You could knock the door down if necessary. As you might expect, entering a location after you have knocked the door down could be problematic. You don't know what is on the other side of the door. Even though you wear gear that has POLICE written on it and shouting police as you enter, anything could go wrong and sometimes does.

We obtained a search warrant for a location in the 1200 block of Charles Street in downtown Baltimore. We had watched the house for several nights before getting the warrant. We had observed a lot of male traffic going in and out of this house from the hours of 11 P.M. until 3 A.M. All the men were white and appeared to be middle age or older.

When we would hit a house for anything, we always made sure we had enough manpower. You never knew what would happen. On this night, it was my sergeant and my partner who were serving the search warrant with me. Pete was the sergeant in charge and Joe was my partner. Early in the night we had solicited the help of a couple guys who were working in the drug unit. We had Sergeant Leon Tomlin and one of his men, Vernon Wilhelm.

We went to the house at about 11 P.M. and watched the house for a while. We did see a couple of men leave and a couple enter the house. We decided to hit the house, knowing the prostitute was there and probably a trick.

I have to describe Sergeant Leon Tomlin for you to get a picture of his size. He was six foot five and weighed every bit of two hundred and seventy pounds. I had seen him knock down some doors in the past. I don't think he ever met the door he couldn't take down with one blow. As big as he was, he was extremely agile. Leon went on to be a colonel in the police department. He was a great street cop and admired by everyone.

The plan was that Leon would knock the door down. The rest of us would all enter the property and hope for the best.

Well, here is what happened...Leon knocked down the door as planned. The rest of us ran in the house hollering *POLICE*. We had gotten in the house so fast that we were in the rear bedroom in seconds. When we entered the room, we saw a man in bed on top of a female. He was having sex and did not stop when we were in the room. The female appeared to be struggling to push the man off because she could see us. The man had his back to us. I have to describe the man for you to get a good feeling of why we were standing in the room laughing our asses off. He was an elderly man, mostly bald, skinny, and did not have any pants on. He had a bowling shirt on with large letters on the back that read...*LUCKY STRIKES*. On the sleeve of the shirt he had a patch that read, *300 GAME*.

98

The female was scared to death. We had to actually pull this guy off the girl. When he realized what was happening, he started to hold his chest. Seeing how old the guy was, we tried to calm him down or he probably would have had a heart attack. We sat him in a chair. It appeared that he could not understand what we were saying. I leaned in to talk to him and tell him that everything would be all right. That's when I saw that he was wearing hearing aids. Hell, the poor man couldn't hear us when we knocked down the door. He couldn't even hear us when we were hollering *POLICE*. That's why he didn't stop the dirty deed.

After a few minutes, we had the whole room laughing. The prostitute, the old man, and every cop in the room could not control their laughter. Even the prostitute who knew she was getting arrested thought the whole thing was hilarious.

We took the guy outside for some air. Normally, we would have arrested the poor guy. The more we talked to him, we felt sorry for him. He said that he had bowled earlier in the night. He came to the whorehouse to get laid. He said that he had been frequenting this house for several months. I was starting to be proud of the old guy. We told him we would take his name and let him go. We did tell him he would have to show up in court. He agreed and begged us not to call his wife. He said that his wife was ill and something like this would probably kill her.

We let him go and I have always wondered if he had ever told this story to his bowling buddies.

Let me end with a bowling message to that nice old man...

"Why do prostitutes prefer to have sex instead of bowling?

Because the balls are lighter, and you don't have to change your shoes.

I've got to get my mind out of the gutter...spare me please.

Conversation # 19

Allow me to have one more conversation about working in the Vice Unit.

This story is about a situation that occurred in a massage parlor. As I have said before, working vice entails all kinds of illegal activity. In the Central District, which is in the heart of downtown Baltimore City, there were several massage parlors that opened. I can assure you that most of them were a front for prostitution or other illegal activity. The money these places were making was quite substantial. When you watched the activity entering and leaving in a short period of time, you knew that something other than massages were going on.

We had several complaints about these so-called massage parlors from people who lived in the area where the parlors sprung up. They were everywhere and were being operated by a person you could probably call a manager or more appropriately a madam. The clients who frequented the parlors would call and make an appointment through the madam.

Let's clear up something before I go any further; the people performing the massages in these parlors were not board certified or a masseuse of any kind. A massage therapist who is board certified is trained to do manual manipulation of soft body tissue to enhance a person's health and well-being. The ladies in these so-called massage parlors performed some manipulation, but it was not on any soft body tissue. They performed something on a man's best friend...if you know what I mean.

As these massage parlors were sprouting up everywhere, our captain ordered us to close down as many as possible. You remember my sergeant, Pete Bailey, from previous conversations and my partner, Joe Bolesta. We knew that the only way to make an arrest was to make an appointment at the parlor and see what was going on inside.

We decided to start with one that we knew had a lot of activity. We knew this by watching the place and observing men entering and leaving in a short period of time. The massage parlor was located in a residential neighborhood. They had taken over an old storefront and set up the massage parlor. The plan was for two of us to make an appointment for the same time. We would go in the place as if we didn't know each other. We knew this could be a touchy situation.

In this type of assignment, you could not carry your gun, badge, or anything that made you look like a cop. The other reason that made it dangerous was that we knew that these places probably had a man on the premise to protect the ladies.

Pete decided that he and I would make the appointments. We both called at separate times. It was easy getting the appointment. The lady answering the phone said it would be thirty dollars for a partial or fifty dollars for a full massage. Not sure what the difference was between the two. We both said we wanted the full massage.

With the appointments made, we talked about strategy and any problems that might come up. The plan was to actually get on the massage table. If we got propositioned for any type of sex act, we would make the arrest. Once we were solicited for a sex act, we would identify ourselves as police officers. Now, this involved some timing issues; would I get propositioned before Pete or would he be first. We figured that if it was going to happen, it would happen fairly quick. We knew they would have a lot of customers to get to.

We decided we would enter the place about five minutes apart and get on a table as quick as possible. Hopefully we would be in the same area so we could at least hear each other when announcing an arrest. We decided that Joe and a couple of uniformed officers would be parked outside nearby. Pete told Joe to give us about twenty minutes from the time we entered the place before they came in.

With everything in place, Pete went in first. I went in about five minutes later. We were told to sit in the lobby and wait for a girl to perform the massage. Pete, as I have told you was a real character; he was always kidding around. While we were waiting, he played it like he didn't know me. He started to talk to me as if I were a stranger. I guess he did it for the effect on the receptionist.

Pete said, "Hi guy, you come here often?"

Well, I did everything I could to keep from busting out laughing. With the receptionist watching, I needed to respond.

"No, this is my first time. Have you been here before?"

I was worried that the receptionist would pick up on us trying not to laugh.

A door opened and a very attractive lady who appeared to be about thirty years old walked over to us and asked who was next. I knew I had to get away from Pete, so I jumped up and said, "Can I go first? I have to get back to work."

Pete, stood up and said, "That's fine, you can take him; I took the whole day off to come here."

I followed this lady back through a corridor with small rooms on both sides. I couldn't see in the rooms as there was a curtain drawn closed on each room. I was thinking that the twenty minutes might be up soon and Joe and the troops will be coming through the door screaming POLICE, before we get propositioned. I was also thinking that when Pete comes back, would he be close enough to me to hear me say anything.

When we got halfway down the corridor, the female told me to go in a room. She told me to put on the robe hanging on the door. I guess I shocked her when I asked if I should take off all my clothes. She laughed and said, "Honey, if you want the fifty-dollar massage, you need to be completely naked?"

I'm not sure why, but I felt a little uncomfortable. I knew what I had to do. I felt naked without a gun and badge. Now, I have to take off all my clothes. What the hell could go wrong with this picture?

I undressed and put on the robe. The robe looked like it had been used before. While I was adjusting the robe, the female walked in. She told me her name; it was Windy...not Wendy, but Windy. She asked if I had a problem with the robe and before I could answer, she said, "Honey, this ain't a fuckin hospital, you want the massage on not?"

I got on the table with the robe still on. I was hoping she would proposition me for a sex act so we could get this over with. I was surprised when she actually started to massage my shoulders. She was using some kind of greasy stuff that smelled like oranges. I wasn't sure where this was going to go, but, it started to feel good. She then asked me to roll over. She opened the robe. I was thinking, *maybe this broad is really giving me a massage.*

Well, it finally happened, she starting asking what I liked from women. I told her that I liked everything possible from a woman.

I will tell you that she was direct and to the point. She said she would give me the best blow job I ever had. With that, she reached down and grabbed me by the private parts. I mean she grabbed me so hard that I came halfway up off the table.

I knew this was time to identify myself as a police officer and make the arrest. I got off the table. I really did get off the table and grabbed her by the arm. I told her she was under arrest for soliciting for a perverted sex act. She started screaming and ran out of the small cubicle, with me in pursuit...naked.

While she was screaming, I could see guys coming out of the other cubicles. They were running with their clothes in their hands. I kept yelling...*POLICE* and she kept running. Now I'm wondering...*where the hell is Pete? Where is the backup that was supposed to come through the door?*

Well, my wish was granted; Joe and the uniform guys came in the place. They were hollering...*POLICE* and the place was in complete mayhem. I grabbed the girl I was chasing as she almost got out the back door. If you can picture this, I'm holding a scantily clad female and I ain't got no clothes on. *Where in the hell is Pete?*

As I'm walking toward the front of the place, I see Pete in the hallway. He's half naked. Believe me, it was not a pretty sight. I told one of the uniform men to hold the girl, so I could go put my clothes on. When I got back and was dressed, I asked Pete what happened with the female he had.

As I told you before, Pete was a real character. He rarely told the truth. At first, he wouldn't tell me what happened; he just kept laughing at me for chasing Windy down the hallway. He told the uniform officers that they would never see anything like this the rest of their career in law enforcement. He was probably right.

We arrested Windy, the manager of the parlor, and the guy we figured was a bouncer type of guy. We were going to arrest all the girls in the place, but we decided we had the best case on Windy and the manager.

Later after we placed the charges on everyone, I asked Pete to be serious and tell me what happened. He said, "Well, I put on the robe and got on the table. She started to rub my back and neck. I was thinking, damn, this feels so good. She was really rubbing me hard. She was talking about how she got involved in the massage business. She was telling me about her kids. She said what she was doing was easy money; it supported her family. She rolled me over and was rubbing my chest. She never stopped talking. I was feeling sorry for her. I think she was just about to proposition me, when I heard some asshole running down the hallway hollering *POLICE*. She ran out the door and that's when all the screaming and chasing started. I don't know where she got to. I assume she ran out the back door."

"Pete, I don't believe a thing you said and furthermore, that asshole hollering *POLICE* was me. Did you forget the plan or did you fall in love with the girl? I don't need to know anymore, because I don't believe a word you say."

 For the rest of the day and days to come, it was a standing joke to tell anyone that would listen about how I was running down the hallway naked trying to catch the massage girl. There are times in police work that stories like this have a tendency to spread throughout the department. I can honestly tell you that I have heard this story so many times over the years. I know who is responsible for spreading the story...his name is Pete.

I love and hate Pete. I can honestly say that as I look back on my years working with both Pete and Joe, were the most exciting and rewarding times I had in the police department. We did the job. We also had a hell of lot of fun.

Maybe one day in a moment of weakness, Pete will tell me the truth about what actually happened that day, although I have a pretty good idea.

I do remember that fat ass, naked, middle-aged, sergeant coming out of the room with a smile on his face.

I guess we can just chalk it up as one for the good guys.

Conversation # 20

Now that we've talked in much detail about my trials and tribulations working in the Vice Unit, let's move on to my time in the Homicide Unit.

If you know anything about police work, you would know that being selected to work in such a prestigious unit as the Homicide Unit is an honor and a privilege. In most police agencies, only the cream of the crop gets selected to work in a Homicide Unit. I'm not bragging; it's just a fact in law enforcement.

I can remember when I came on the police department, I was fascinated by the homicide detectives. When they came out on a murder scene they were always dressed in suits, long overcoats, and many wore hats. They wore Stetson hats; the type that my dad wore when I was a kid. I was always star-struck by those detectives. I knew early on in my career that one day I wanted to be in that unit.

For me to be selected for assignment to the Homicide Unit with only eight years on the job, was one of the biggest accomplishments in my law enforcement career.

In my first book, I talked in much detail about a man that lived in my neighborhood when I was growing up. His name was Jim Cadden. I also talked about him earlier in this book. Jim was a World War II veteran and a member of the Army's 101st Airborne. He fought in numerous battles in the war, including the *Battle of The Bulge*. He received a *silver star,* three *bronze stars* and two *purple hearts*. When he came home from the war he was a hero in our neighborhood.

I can remember in the 1950s as a young kid, I would see him walking in the neighborhood and everyone would want to talk to him. He was the type of person that by the way he carried himself, he exuded confidence and therefore received the respect that he deserved. He was a tough guy in the right way. Although he was a big man, he didn't push his weight around. When he joined the Baltimore City Police Department, I think everybody in our neighborhood knew he was destined for greatness.

From the day I went on the police department, other than my father, Jim Cadden, was the guy I looked up to. I'm not going to bore you with a lot that I have already written about in my first book. At different times in his career, Jim Cadden held every position in the Homicide Unit from detective all the way up to captain.

When I got assigned to the Homicide Unit in 1973, he was the captain. I had worked hard to get to the Homicide Unit. Knowing Captain Cadden and coming from the same neighborhood seemed to push it along a little quicker.

I remember when I first walked into the Homicide Unit. My sergeant told me that the captain wanted to see me after roll call. I was really nervous as I walked back to his office. Even though I knew this man from the old neighborhood, he was now my captain.

I felt like I had come full circle...from a kid admiring him for his service in the war, to now actually working under his command. The meeting didn't last long. Cadden was a man of few words. He was the type of guy that when he spoke, he was very clear on what he wanted to get across. He wished me well and told me that if I ever needed anything to come to him. As I was leaving his office, he stopped me, put his hand on my shoulder and said, "Richard, you come from good stock. Your father was an inspiration to me when I first joined the department. He was like a mentor. I want to pay that back, so if you need anything, do not hesitate to come to me."

I thanked him and in typical Captain Cadden fashion he said, "Now get out there and solve some murders."

Looking back on my time in the Homicide Unit, I consider it a privilege to have worked for so many years in that unit.

On the wall of the roll call room was a large plaque that read...*No greater honor can be bestowed on a human being than to investigate the death of another human being.*

Now, you want to guess who put that plaque there...you're right, it was Captain Cadden.

I worked with some tremendous investigators in the years that I spent in homicide. I could go on writing forever about them, but I might skip someone and that would not be justice.

My first boss, Sergeant Rod Brandner, was probably the guy who made the biggest impression on me. Rod was an excellent investigator and a good supervisor. I learned so much from him. He was not just your supervisor; he was a very good friend. He led by example and knew when to put some levity into the job. Rod was a real prankster; you had to be on your toes with him. I look back on those days working in his squad with fond memories. I think he pulled those pranks to keep us loose. He knew that working murders everyday could take a toll on you both physically and mentally.

I could talk about guys like, my first partner in homicide, Frank Perkowski. Frank was a great homicide detective; he didn't miss anything on a crime scene. He always kept me straight with our report writing. He would always search for new words to put in the report. I think he just wanted to mess with the bosses. I often think that because of his excellent writing skills, it may have rubbed off on me.

Frank had this stern look on him. You couldn't tell what mood he was in on any day. That mood paid off on many interrogations of murder suspects. Frank would walk around the conference table and put his hand on the murder suspect's shoulder. In a tone of voice that sounded like a priest, he would say, *I can see that you're hurting inside. I know you want to tell us about the murder. Just relax and let in out, you will feel relieved.*

I saw this happen on many occasions, but when I tried it, it didn't work. I think Frank and I worked the good guy-bad guy routine about as good as anyone in the unit. I was the bad guy. When I saw that Frank's approach was not working, I would burst into the interview room hollering and screaming. Frank would put his hand on my shoulder and tell me to relax. I would leave the room and Frank would assure the suspect that he would not allow me back in the room. If Frank didn't win the guy over and get a confession, I would repeat my act and beat on the door. I would holler that I was coming in and taking over the interview. I will always remember when Frank got the confession; he would come out of the room and say, *we got him sox, now you can go in and holler at him for a while.*

There were so many others in the Homicide Unit that were really good at what they did. As I mentioned earlier, you had to be a well-rounded detective to stay in that unit. There was no room in the unit for anyone that could not hold their weight. It was a job that you could not worry about going home on time. You might have a murder on a Thursday and not go home until Sunday.

As you might expect, the divorce rate in the unit was very high and that included me.

Another detective that was a legend in the unit was Furrie Cousins. Furrie was a man that had put twenty years in the unit. When I first came to homicide, he took me under his wing. On the night shift when things were quiet, which was not that often, he would talk to me about murder investigations. He would go over old case files to show me what others had done on some of the more involved murders. He didn't give me any slack on his questions. He actually got mad when I didn't know something that was apparently obvious to him.

I remember going out on a murder with Furrie when I only had about a month in the unit. His regular partner was off and he picked me to go with him. He could have picked anyone of the other more experienced detectives. He told the sergeant, "I'm taking this rook with me. I want to see what he's got."

He then threw the keys to the car at me. I knew that I was not only going to be his driver; I was going to be his student at the murder investigation. I remember the murder very vividly; it was a decomposed body of a man. It was in July and extremely hot. The body was found in an apartment in midtown Baltimore City.

When we arrived on the scene, the emergency unit officers told us that the smell was extremely bad in the apartment. When you smell a decomposed body in a very hot room in July, you will never forget it. They suggested that we put on plastic jump suits and wear gloves. Well, Furrie laughed at this suggestion. He told me and the others on the scene that we don't need any jumpsuits or gloves. He told them that we are homicide investigators and this is what we do for a living. I was actually halfway into the plastic suit when he said that. I pulled my legs out of the suit so fast that I almost fell over.

We went in the house and up to the second floor. As we climbed the stairs, you could start to smell the odor from the decomposed body. The smell was new to me, but I was sure that Furrie had experienced the smell many times before. I had heard from some detectives that when you have a *stinker,* you should light a cigar and keep it in your mouth. I didn't have any cigars and I was not about to ask Furrie if he had any. As I was basically along for the ride, I waited to see what Furrie would do. Even though he was just a detective, the uniformed officers knew him and treated him as if he was a boss. He stood there with his notepad and just looked around the room. I followed suit and I think that the uniform officers picked up on the fact that I was new. After taking some notes, Furrie said, "These maggots didn't kill this guy. What do you think rook?"

Before I could even attempt to give an answer, he said, "Let's get down here closer and see what we can find."

He knelt directly over the body and motioned for me to do the same. He turned to the uniform officer and told him that we would now need gloves. We both put on plastic gloves. Furrie told me that he thought the guy was shot in the head. I didn't question him, but I didn't see any holes in the head. There were so many maggots and dried blood, I really couldn't see much. Furrie pushed some of the maggots away from the side of the head and sure as shit, I could see a hole in the guy's head. What happened next, I will never forget as long as I live.

Furrie told me to stick my finger in the hole in the man's head. He said that he would stick his finger in the other side. I'm not sure if he was screwing with me or not. He said that if our fingers met, it would confirm that the bullet was a through and through shot. He said that this meant that the bullet went in one side and out the other. I don't know where I got the courage, but I reached down and brushed some maggots away. I stuck my finger in the bullet hole. I think I was kind of turning my head away, but I could not feel his finger.

Furrrie laughed and stood up. I was waiting for some kind of explanation on why we couldn't touch fingers. Furrie liked to play to the crowd. We had about five officers in the room and they were looking at Furrie like he was a college professor. Loud enough for everyone to hear, he said, "You passed your first test by putting your finger in his head. You failed the second test, because there is no way in hell our fingers could touch "

With all eyes and ears on him from the room full of uniformed officers, he was giving me a lesson. He went on to say that there was no way our fingers could meet because there is brain matter still in the head. He said that even though the bullet went in one side and came out the other side, the velocity of the bullet coming from the weapon would be a clean entry but would not remove or disturb enough brain matter that we could have touched fingers.

At first, I was a little pissed that he was apparently mocking me in front of the uniform officers. But, after a few minutes, I figured it was probably a good lesson after all. I was new and learning on the job. We finished the scene investigation and headed back to the office.

When we were driving back to the office, he told me that he was not mocking me. He said that what he told me about the velocity of a bullet in the head was true and there would be no doubt that I would see it again in the future.

We worked that murder for about three weeks. I learned a lot from Furrie that helped me during my later years in the Homicide Unit.

The outcome of the investigation was that the man had gone down *The Block*. I told you about *The Block* earlier. He mistakenly picked up what he thought were two females, but they were female impersonators. They all went to the impersonators apartment where they robbed and killed him. It was a sad case because the man was a wealthy man from the suburbs of Baltimore. He was sixty-six years old and died a very violent death.

These kinds of murders were always tough to explain to the family. I found out over a period of time from Furrie and others that the best way to convey to the family what happened to their loved one, was to simply tell the truth and tell it quick. The reasoning behind telling someone about a murder quick was that if you beat around the bush with small talk, most families knew what was coming. If you told them quickly, the hollering, screaming, and crying would start. Telling them what happened was out there without a bunch of beating around the bushes.

Over the years, I have seen family members do some unbelievable things when told about a murder. I saw a victim's sister run about twenty feet toward a window in the homicide office and jump into the window. If the window had not been unbreakable, she would have plunged six stories to the ground.

This victim in the murder I worked with Furrie was the vice president of the family owned business. We had the whole family together when Furrie and I told them what happened. They had a lot of questions and we answered all of them...except the part about the fingers in the head. I'm not sure how they would have handled that. I guess I could have told them it was just a training exercise.

Another bizarre story about my homicide days:

We got a call to respond to investigate an attempted suicide. We went to the location which was a three-story rowhouse in Baltimore City. When we pulled up we could see a rope hanging from the second floor of the house. When we talked to the uniform officers, they could hardly talk through their laughter.

The story conveyed to us was that the victim, a man in his late fifties, tied a rope around his neck. He jumped out of the second-floor window of a three-story rowhouse. We soon found out why all the laughing; the guy jumped from a window that was about thirty feet from the ground. The problem was he had fifty feet of rope.

When the uniform officers arrived, the man was on the sidewalk in his underwear with the rope still around his neck. He was taken to Mercy Hospital.

Because the guy was alive, we wanted to talk to him. We wanted to find out what his reason was for jumping. We didn't have to continue with any investigation because he was alive...we were the Homicide Unit, not the make a fool out of yourself unit.

We went to the hospital and talked to the guy. He was being treated for a broken leg, broken ribs, broken wrist, and multiple bruises all over his body. He was actually very lucky. If he had hit his head, the doctor said he probably would have died...thus completing his original mission.

When we went in the room, he was awake. He looked really bad...*no shit, he had just jumped out the second-floor window in a miserable attempt to kill himself.*

He was hollering and crying at the same time. He kept saying, "Why the fuck can't I kill myself?"

He repeated it over and over. My partner on this call was Frank Perkowski. Like I said earlier, Frank had one expression and that didn't change much no matter what the situation was. When the guy stopped screaming, Frank leaned in to the bed and in classic Frank style said, "Listen dude, if you want to try to kill yourself in the future, make sure you don't jump out a window that's thirty feet off the ground, with fifty feet of rope."

The guy started crying again and we left the room...

Another story about my homicide days...

Let me tell you a story about a good friend and former homicide detective. I told you how Frank Perkowski never changed his expressions. Well, this guy I'm going to tell you about might be worse than Frank. You never knew where he was coming from. He was a good investigator. He always seemed like he wanted to be somewhere else. I know he loved working in homicide, but you would never know it from his demeanor. Nothing bothered this guy; he was about as carefree as anyone I have ever known. His name is Ronnie Mikles and the story goes like this:

As I have mentioned earlier in other conversations, we worked hard in the Homicide Unit. We partied hard also. The two never mixed. When we were on the clock working murders, we were one of the finest homicide units in the country. Our clearance rate was very high. We were recognized as one of the best. We frequently trained other police department Homicide Units.

Mikles and I worked in the same squad. We were not partners. When one of our partners was on leave, we did hook up to work some murder investigations. As much as this guy was a strange dude at work, he was even stranger when we were out drinking.

You never knew what he would do after a few drinks. An example would be like the time we were in a nice restaurant in downtown Baltimore. It was probably considered at that time a very upscale restaurant and bar. It had a piano player in the bar area and the clientele were always dressed very nice.

One night we were sitting at the bar having some drinks. I noticed Mikles walking around the bar. He was stopping to talk to people. I found this very strange. He was not the kind to seek out conversations from strangers. He returned to sit next to me and then the strangest thing happened.

A guy, a very big guy, tapped me on the shoulder. When I turned around, he put his finger in my chest. At first, I thought I knew the guy, but that changed quickly. He poked me again in the chest and said, "I hear you're a Marine. I was told that you're a judo expert. I don't think you look like a very tough guy."

Well, I was shocked for a minute, but knew I better say something before this guy sucker punched me. I tried to stand up. He was so big, I couldn't move. I glanced over at Mikles and he was giggling, which I thought was strange. If there was going to be a fight, I would not want my buddy sitting there giggling.

I managed to get up from the barstool. I maneuvered into a position of defense in case we started to fight. The guy did not appear that he was ready to throw a punch, but he was big and scary looking. I had a couple of drinks, but I was very aware of what could be going down. The guy looked at Mikles and then back at me. He said, "Your buddy here told me that you like to get into fights. Well, I'm here anytime you want to try me out."

When he said that, I knew that Mikles had talked to the guy. He had put that shit in the guy's head about judo and liking to fight. I told the guy that I'm not a judo guy and I don't look for fights, especially with a guy his size. The guy started to laugh and that was a good thing. He slapped Mikles on the back and walked away. Well, I was furious; I told Mikles that his childish acts are going to backfire on him one day. He's going to get somebody hurt.

I stayed drinking with Mikles for the rest of the night. We left that location and went to a few more bars. About 1 A.M. in the morning, I wanted to go home. Mikles was insisting that we go to another bar. He was drunk and refusing to let me take him home. I didn't know where he lived, but I knew the general area. I drove and kept asking him for his address. He refused to even talk to me. After a while, he fell asleep in my car. I mean he was out like a light.

I was driving around and was getting pissed that I didn't know where to take him. I drove by a cemetery and the gate was open. I drove into the cemetery and parked on a small road next to several gravesites. He was still asleep and I had enough with this guy's silly shit all night.

I opened the car door on his side and pulled him out. I thought sure he would wake up, but he didn't. I literally dragged him across the short road and placed him next to a tombstone. I propped him up in the sitting position. He actually looked comfortable. Knowing that he lived in the general area, I just thought I would leave him there. When he woke up, he could just walk home. It was really dark and creepy in the cemetery. If anyone had seen me dragging Mikles, they would have sworn he was dead.

Before I left him, I took his gun and badge. I was going to take his wallet but decided to leave that on him. The entire time I was dragging him and taking his gun and badge, he didn't wake up at all. He was out cold and didn't make any sounds. I drove out of the cemetery and went home. On the way, I was thinking about going back to get him. I decided, the hell with him. He had messed with me earlier in the bar and almost got my ass kicked...screw him.

I went home and went to bed. I did think about him and what the hell he would do when he woke up next to a tombstone.

That same day I was working the 4 PM to midnight shift. I got to work in time for roll call. I didn't see Mikles and that worried me. Was he still asleep next to the tombstone? Did he fall into a grave and had a heart attack when he woke up? Did someone see him and call the police? Did he wake up and walk home? Was he totally pissed at me? Would he want to beat the shit out of me when he saw me? I'm pretty sure the one about kicking my ass would be the correct one.

After roll call, I asked the sergeant about Mikles. He said that he had called in and said he would be a little late for work. When I heard that, I was getting scared. Did he think I dropped him there and someone took his gun and badge? Well, I didn't have to wait long for the answer. He came in the office and had the look he always had, but this time it was a deeper darkness in his expression. I wanted to say something, but I decided to wait it out.

After he took his coat off and got a coffee, he walked over to me. He got right up in my face. He paused for a minute. He then, very calmly and in a low tone said, "You better have my gun and badge. What the fuck kind of joke was that to leave me in a fuckin graveyard...are you nuts?"

I gave him his gun and badge. I tried to avoid him for a while until he cooled down. He started to approach me again. I put my hand up and said, "You think I'm nuts? How about all the crazy shit you have pulled on me and others in the unit. Last night you almost got me killed by that big bastard that you told I was a judo expert and loved to fight. I tried to take you home, but you wouldn't tell me where you lived. What was I supposed to do?"

He walked away and I knew he was pissed. I knew it would take a while for him to come around. He was sitting at his desk and hollered all the way across the room, "You could have taken me to your house to sleep. Who the fuck drops their friend off in a graveyard, takes their gun and badge, and goes home to sleep? I'll get you back for this you bastard."

By the end of the shift that night, the entire squad knew the story. Every time Mikles walked by them, they would ask questions about his night in the graveyard. He didn't talk to me for a few days.

It turned out to be one of those stories that got told over and over when we were out drinking. The story got embellished to the extent that they had me putting Mikles in a grave and throwing dirt on him to keep him warm.

All these years later, when we are at retirement meetings, parties, funerals, or getting together for breakfast...I am always asked to tell the story about putting Mikles in the cemetery. We are very good friends today. We still laugh about what happened those many years ago.

I know I have said one more story a few times. I promise, we are moving along.

While I'm still conversing about the Homicide Unit, I must talk about the homicide softball team. I was the manager of the team. Not sure how I got that position, I guess no one else wanted it. My job was to schedule some games, make sure we had enough players, make the line-up, keep everyone happy, and make sure we had enough beer at the games.

We had a good team, even though most of our players were always much older than our opponents. We had guys ranging in age from the early '30s to the late '50s. Don't get me wrong, we had some good players; guys that had played softball most of their adult life.

We had a couple of home run hitters, but for the most part we were single hitters. A couple of our older guys could get a single whenever needed. They had that ability, which often proved better in softball.

Most of our games were played against patrol districts, some specialized units, and the States Attorney's Office. The most competitive games I remember were with the States Attorney's Office. It was a rivalry that at times got a little heated. We were friends with all the attorneys because we were in court often with the murder trials.

As I remember it, and I can be corrected by an attorney from back in those days, the Homicide Unit won most of the games. It seemed like we always got behind early and then in the later innings, we would score and win the game.

My job as the manager was not easy. Most of our guys were older, but they still had that fire in them and wanted to play. I did my best to get everyone in the game. I also took it seriously and always wanted to win. On some occasions, I had to leave the starters in the game. I caught hell for it later at the bar.

Speaking of the bar, it was a tradition that after a game, no matter who we played, we went to Bo Brooks Crab House to drink. Bo Brooks sponsored our team and paid for the uniforms. Most of our games were on Thursdays after work. After the game, we would get to the bar around 8 P.M. and would usually close the place. A lot of guys would try to take off on Friday. Some guys would call in late with some lame excuse; it was really the late-night drinking.

I really don't know how I got to be the manager. I did have a little help from a couple of the older guys who didn't play. They loved to be at the games. My helpers were, Charlie Kropfelter and Joe Powell. Both were excellent ball players in their day. After the games that we lost, I knew that I would get an earful from both of them later at the bar. I always listened to these guys because they had been around for a while and were usually right. After a couple beers, if they were still giving me some heat, I would politely tell them to get the hell off my back. Even the day after a game, they would seek me out in the homicide office to talk about why we lost.

We had some real characters on the team. When we first started to play other teams, we always had a cooler of beer at the game. I actually had guys come to me in the middle innings and ask to be taken out of the game. I knew why they wanted out; it was to drink some beer on a hot summer night. We had some wives and girlfriends come to our games. I don't think they cared much for me. I think they didn't like me because I took their husband or boyfriend out of the game.

I remember one game when the other team scored nine runs on our pitcher in the first inning. I went to the mound and took him out of the game. When I got back to the sideline, his girlfriend approached me. She was furious. She got up in my face and said, "Why did you take him out?"

Well, I was never really a guy who held back what I wanted to say. I got back in her face and said, "Did you see the nine runs the other team scored? I took him out because he's getting bombed out there. If you want to manage the team, here's the clipboard; if not, sit down and shut up!"

I also had a player on the team who was a pretty good outfielder and he just happened to be my brother, John. We both worked in the Homicide Unit at the same time, which was unusual. It had only happened one other time that I remember. John was real character and an excellent softball player. He was a single guy and played to a different drummer than most people.

I remember on one occasion, we were winning by a few runs. I decided to take John out of the game. He was playing right field. I sent a guy out to right field to replace him. John refused to come out of the game, so I had two players in right field. The umpire stopped the game. He told me to get one of them off the field. I motioned for John to come off the field. He just laughed and stayed there. I went halfway out in the field to talk to him. He said, "I ain't coming out. I came here today to play the whole game; take somebody else out."

I was really pissed at him, but what could I do. The umpire was hollering that he would end the game and give the win to the other team. I left the field and didn't talk to him the rest of the game and even later at the bar.

I got a lot of crazy stories about John. I'll hold them for now because we have to keep moving along.

We were in a softball tournament in Aberdeen, Maryland. We went up on a Friday and played one game in the evening. We won the game and knew we would play at least two more games on Saturday.

Friday night the host team held a cookout at the local FOP (Fraternal Order of Police) lodge. The beer was flowing. After the cookout, it continued at a local bar. I was drinking along with the rest of them, but I stopped around midnight. I tried to get the guys to leave and get some sleep for the games the following day. It didn't work. The team stayed out and drank well into the early morning of Saturday.

Our first game on Saturday was set for 10 A.M. I was at the field along with three guys from our team at 9:30 A.M. As game time approached, four more guys showed up. They looked really bad. Just a few minutes before 10 A.M., we had nine players and that included me. We didn't take any infield practice or any warmups. The umpire asked me if we were ready to start. I told him I was waiting for one more player; you needed ten to field a team. The umpire said he would give me five minutes and then he would have to forfeit the game to our opponent. Just at the five-minute mark, the tenth player showed up. I knew just by the look on this guy, he was hungover.

The game started and it was not pretty. We couldn't field any balls, the pitcher was wild, the outfielders either dropped balls or didn't even get close to them. We actually had one player in center field come in on a high fly ball; it hit him on the top of the head. Instead of chasing the ball, he threw his glove down and started cursing the ball.

In softball, they have what they call the *slaughter rule*. The rule means if a team scores eleven runs in an inning, the game is over. Well, our opponent scored ten runs in the first inning. We came to bat and didn't score in the first, second, or third inning. We did eventually score four runs and lost the game seventeen to four.

We were scheduled to play in the losers' bracket at 2 P.M. that day. I told the guys to go get lunch and sober up. I was so mad. I couldn't even have lunch with them. I was hoping that the few hours they had before the next game would make a difference and we could at least leave Aberdeen with a little pride.

We did win the afternoon game. I guess that was some consolation for the disgraceful way we played in the morning game. We could have easily won that tournament. I know our guys were much better than the opponents. It goes to show you that alcohol and athletics don't mix.

Conversation # 21

In the Homicide Unit of the Baltimore City Police Department, a high-profile murder investigation was called a *Red Ball*.

Not sure how that name came about; it was a way of distinguishing it from the normal everyday murders in Baltimore City. Not long after the initial on-scene murder investigation, the term *Red Ball* would be tagged to the investigation. It remained that way until the murder was either solved or moved over to the Cold Case Unit.

In 1982, my squad got one of the most unusual *Red Ball* murders that you could ever imagine. Most of your murders in a high crime city like Baltimore, occur on the street. This murder occurred on the death row cellblock of the Maryland Penitentiary; that's right, you heard me right...a murder on death row.

I was a supervisor of one of the six homicide squads within the Homicide Unit of the Baltimore City Police Department. My squad consisted of six very experienced detectives. Most had at least five years in the unit; a few had over ten years. I had been in the Homicide Unit since 1974 as a detective. In 1978, I got promoted to sergeant. After one year in patrol, I returned to the Homicide Unit as a detective sergeant.

The procedure for handling new murders in the unit went like this: when the phone rang in the office and it was the police dispatcher informing us of a murder, the squad that was next up took the murder. The detective answering the phone would not necessarily get the assignment. The investigation would go to the detective who was up next. Up next meant that if you were working and it was your turn, you got the assignment. When you got the assignment, another detective would be assigned as the secondary and you would be the lead detective on the murder investigation.

Red Ball murders would get more attention than your normal everyday murder. All the murders in Baltimore did get thoroughly investigated. Because the media would be hungry for information on high profile murders, the *Red Ball* murders got the most attention. The detectives in the unit took pride in solving all murders. When you were assigned a *Red Ball* murder, you felt like you had to up your game a little because you had many eyes on what you did.

It was something about working murder investigations that consumed your everyday thoughts and action. You would work the case during your shift and when you got home, it was still on your mind.

There is a TV show called, *First 48 Hours*. The premise of the show is that if a murder investigation was not solved in forty-eight hours, it was a strong possibility that it would not be solved. I agree with the premise of the show. From my experience working in the Homicide Unit in Baltimore, I found this to be true on most murders. That's why our detectives stayed with a murder investigation around the clock for at least the first twenty-four hours. I can remember having detectives in my squad that literally begged me to allow them to keep working on a murder investigation after their shift ended. I know that the overtime money was an incentive. I could see the fire and tenacity in them to just catch the murder suspect.

Remember, I told you about the plaque on the wall in the office that read:

NO GREATER HONOR COULD BE BESTOWED UPON A HUMAN BEING THAN TO INVESTIGATE THE DEATH OF ANOTHER HUMAN BEING...

We took the words on that plaque very serious.

Along with the dedication of the detectives in the unit, there was the ever-present homicide board. The board, which took up a whole wall in the sergeant's room, contained the names of every person that was murdered in the city during the current year. The names on the board in black were solved cases. The names that were in red were the unsolved cases. The names in blue were cases that we had obtained a warrant for a suspect. Also, on the board next to the victim's name was the name of the detective handling the case.

If a squad had a lot of red on the board, it would not be long before the sergeant would be called into the lieutenant's office, or sometimes, the captain's office. The talk would be about the progress of the investigations. The board became a bragging point if you had cases in the black. If you had cases in the red, you would get some friendly kidding about not being able to solve the murder.

It was a tradition that on the first day of the new year, the board would be wiped clean. For some that had red on the board, that was a relief. The murders from the previous year did not just go away. Those murders were continuously worked on and if solved, they would go on the board in black, with the year next to the name.

Getting back to the *Red Ball* that I want to write about. In 1982, my squad got the call to meet patrol officers at the Maryland Penitentiary. As this has been many years ago, the exact date is not important. The police dispatcher who called the Homicide Unit informed us that we were needed at the penitentiary for a possible murder on the death row tier of the prison. Knowing this would definitely be a *Red Ball* investigation, I went with the detective to the prison. The detective assigned was a very experienced investigator in the unit.

We arrived at the prison and we were met by a prison official with the rank of captain. He informed us that his guards heard a commotion on the death row tier. When they went to investigate, they observed an inmate hanging from a sheet in his cell. The sheet was configured into a rope, which was around the inmate's neck. The guards cut the sheet down from the ceiling. The inmate was pronounced dead on the scene. Initially, the guards believed that the inmate may have committed suicide. Upon examining the body, they observed numerous wounds that were consisted with a beating. The medical staff at the prison responded to the tier and pronounced the inmate dead. The captain ordered that the body be kept in the cell until our arrival.

Death row at that time consisted of about twenty-five inmates. All but five were waiting to be executed. The other inmates were on the tier serving life sentences without the possibility of parole.

I was very familiar with the Maryland Penitentiary. When growing up, my family lived about two blocks from the penitentiary. I can remember when the executions took place at the prison. The neighbors would gather outside on the street at midnight to watch the lights blink on the top of the prison. On the top of the prison there was a small structure that was used for the executions.

The last person at the prison to be executed by hanging was William Thomas. The hanging occurred on June 10, 1955; I was twelve years old. The last person to die in the gas chamber was Nathaniel Lipscomb on June 9, 1961. I was in the Marine Corps at that time. The last inmates to die by lethal injection were John

Thanos on May 17, 1994, Flint Gregory Hunt on July 2, 1997, Tyrone Gilliam on November 16, 1998, and Steven Oken on June 17, 2004.

Governor Parris Glendening stopped executions by executive order on May 9, 2002. Governor Robert Ehrlich ended the moratorium and resumed executions in 2004. On May 2, 2013, Governor Martin O'Malley signed a law banning executions in Maryland. At that time, Maryland became the eighteenth state in the U.S. to ban the death penalty.

At this point, I would like to explain what we were told and what we observed about life on death row.

When we arrived at the prison we were instructed to put our weapons in a secure location. We knew this procedure from prior visits to correction facilities around the city. We were also advised to leave our wallets, badges, pens, and any other objects that could be used against us by the inmates.

The prison guard in charge of the death row tier told us that the guards do not go on death row. He explained that the inmates' meals are delivered through a secure set of doors. He further explained that the only time the guards would go on the tier would be in an extreme incident where an inmate may be in danger. He said that when they did go on the tier, they went in as a four-man team with full body armor. They had no weapons other than batons and gas grenades. He explained that death row was an entity of its own. It was an isolated, heavily secured, section of the prison. If an inmate needed to come off the tier, he would go through a series of doors with each one locking after he entered it. When he entered the second section, he would remove all his clothing, move to the next section, and then be allowed to put his clothing back on.

After getting some instructions, the captain said that the prison guards would not be accompanying us onto the tier. I found this very unnerving, but we were in their prison and they called the shots. We were told that they would watch us on a closed-circuit monitor. He explained that if needed, the four-man team would come to our rescue. This did not seem like much solace to either of us. We were asked if we had any questions before we went on the tier. I looked at my investigator and we both just shrugged our shoulders. We didn't say anything, but I knew we both had major concerns about our safety.

These inmates were on death row; they were awaiting their execution. What did they have to lose by killing again?

As the guards were preparing to open the series of doors, I can tell you that I was scared. My heart was racing. I could feel the sweat on my back. While we were waiting to go in, our crime lab technician showed up. We briefed him. I can remember him saying, "Are you serious…we're really going in that place?"

As the doors were about to open, I told my investigator and the technician that we needed to go in, ignore the inmates, check the body, take photos, measurements, and get out. The body could be moved later by the Medical Examiner's Office.

As you can imagine, we were not about to ask the death row inmates what happened. Usually on a murder investigation, you would look for witnesses, canvas the area, and just hang around to see if anyone would come forward with information. There would be no hanging around death row. It could be presumed with certainty that most on that tier knew what happened. It could also be presumed that no one would tell us anything.

We entered the tier and went directly to the cell. The victim was on the floor. He still had the sheet around his neck. We observed plenty of blood on the victim which was definitely not consistent with a hanging. Our crime lab tech took photos of the entire cell area. The tier was on a second level of the cellblock that contained approximately twenty cells. We made a cursory examination of the body; noting the marks where there was blood. There was nothing in the cell to recover as evidence, other than the sheet. It appeared that the victim was beaten, probably by more than one person. When he died, they used the sheet to make it look like a suicide.

When we were done in the cell area, we went to the bottom portion of the tier. The technician was attempting to take photos from different angles, having the murder scene included in the photos. He asked one of the inmates if he would move out of the line of the photo. The inmate, a man about six feet five, weighing well over two hundred pounds, with tattoos all over his body, would not move. He used some pretty descriptive nasty language on us and said, "If you want me to move, you'll have to move me!"

The technician looked at me for guidance. Knowing that we were in hostile territory, I told the technician to just move and get a different angle.

As we waited for the photos to be taken, I could hear some rumbling coming from the inmates. I heard one of the inmates say, *he got what he deserved.* I also heard others saying, *what a shame that he had to die.* I knew from the tone of their voices that they were mocking the situation; no one on that tier cared much about what happened.

Nothing can really describe the conditions we observed on death row. I was surprised that it was not filthy, but there was a distinct smell that permeated the entire tier. If I had thought about it earlier, I would have asked that the inmates be placed in their cells while we did our investigation.

The inmates were wandering around and other than some glances, it was as if we were not even there. I noticed that a small ray of sunshine was coming through the top of the tier where there were a few small windows with bars on them. The acoustics were not good. It seemed as if the inmates were all talking at the same time.

As I looked around at the six foot by eight foot cells, I could not help but think, *how in the hell can they keep their sanity in this place.* They were surviving each day under horrible conditions.

The music blared throughout the tier with everything from rock and roll to rap. Most of the music was unintelligible to me, but the inmates seemed to enjoy it. These were hardcore men; most of them had been on death row for long periods of time.

Till this day, I can only imagine what they thought when they started their day...*I'm never getting out, I'm just waiting for the day they kill me.*

Unrelated to the homicide and while we were on the tier, I noticed something really strange for a facility that housed inmates that were going to die or never be released. I watched a guy at the far end of the lower tier selling stuff outside of his cell. It appeared that he was selling candy, cheese crackers, and other small items. Later, when I asked the guard about it, he simply said that they approved the inmate to sell candy and other assorted small items. The guard told me that the inmate's family would bring him the items each week.

The guard started to laugh. He told me that each night when the inmate closed down his little shop, he would walk back to his cell. On several occasions, the inmate got mugged. How ironic, getting mugged on death row, who would ever believe it. The guard told me that the inmate got smart after a couple of muggings. Before the lights went out at night, he would pass his money to a trusted inmate and thus avoid a mugging.

Prior to being moved to death row, the inmate that was murdered was in the main section of the penitentiary. He was described as a tough guy with an attitude. Apparently when he went on the death row tier, he tried to push his weight around and it didn't work. He was no pushover; he was a weightlifter while in the main section. It was obvious from our cursory exam of him in the cell, that he was a well-built man. I would also assume that it would take a few inmates to overcome this guy.

We will never know what really happened. What did this inmate do that would make others want to beat him to death? You have to remember; these inmates were in for horrendous murders. Killing someone that did not fit into their death row lifestyle was not a problem. They know that they're either going to be executed or at the least, they will spend the rest of their life in prison.

The murder was never solved. You can imagine what we were up against trying to solve a murder on death row.

Every time I drive into Baltimore City, I can see the prison from the expressway. The little structure is still on top of the prison. Executions have stopped in Maryland. I don't even know if there is such a place in the prison designated as death row. I would imagine those inmates have been put back in the general population.

It has been many years since that murder. Those inmates that were on death row are very old now, if they are even alive. Wouldn't it be interesting to go into the prison and fined whoever is still alive and see if they will tell us what happened? From my observations back then, I would estimate that the average age of the inmates on death row was probably thirty to thirty-five years. So, many years later, if they are alive, they are in the mid to late sixties or older.

Do they sit around and tell the new inmates about the time a tough, well-built, weightlifter got murdered on death row? Would they remember me and how terrified I must have looked back then?

Since the death penalty in Maryland has been abolished do they now cherish each day? Do they live each day with the thought that death won't come in the little shack on top of the old prison; it will come to them like it comes to everyone...just old age.

Conversation # 22

Is it a homicide, a suicide, or an accidental death? I'll be doggone if we knew.

We got a call one night to meet the patrol officers at a rowhouse in the Patterson Park neighborhood of Southeast Baltimore. The dispatcher told us that the officers were on the scene of a very suspicious death. As I have mentioned before, the Homicide Unit handled: homicides, suicides, accidental deaths, and any death where the patrol officers could not determine how the person died.

When we arrived at the location we talked to the officer. He informed us that the 911 system had received a call from a concerned neighbor. The neighbor reported that he had not seen his friend for several days. He stated that he had made several phone calls to his friend's apartment. He did not get an answer. The neighbor said he had also rapped on his friend's door several times with no response.

The patrol officer stated that believing that something had happened in the apartment, he forced open the door. He said that when he entered the apartment he found a man lying on the kitchen floor completely naked. He was going to call for an ambulance, but it was very obvious from what he saw that the man was deceased.

When my partner, Frank Perkowski, and I entered the apartment we detected a very familiar odor. The odor was that of a body decomposing. The apartment was a toss-up between a hoarder's home or just a complete shithole. The contents of the apartment are hard to describe. There were bottles all over the floor, newspapers just thrown around, plates of food with bugs crawling on the plates, clothes thrown everyway, and just a nasty smell.

Not knowing what we had, we made sure we did not touch or disturb anything. This was one time that not touching or disturbing anything was not only for the integrity of the investigation, but for our own well-being.

When we entered the kitchen, we saw the deceased on the floor. He was a heavyset man and he was naked. Upon examination of the body, we could not

see any wounds above the waist; what we saw below the waist was one of the most horrific sites I had ever seen while working in the Homicide Unit.
We did not have to get down real close to see that the entire scrotum (testicles) and penis were gone. I mean gone, as not there any longer. As we looked even closer, we could see that it appeared that however this happened, it looked like a clean removal of the penis and testes.

We talked more with the patrol officer. He said that a neighbor on the second floor of the house said that the man was obese and was a diabetic. He did not think that the deceased man was employed and he lived alone in the apartment. After we found papers that identified the man, we got a record check. The record check revealed that the deceased was a registered sex offender. It showed that he had criminal charges for molesting minor children. We decided that because of the very strange nature of the condition of the body, we would have the medical examiner respond to the scene.

While waiting for the ME to respond, we talked to some neighbors. It was very clear from talking to the neighbors that they knew the deceased was a sex offender. The people we talked to did not have any love for the deceased. One man we talked to stated that he believed that the deceased was the recipient of many threats in the neighborhood. Another neighbor told us that all the kids in the area were warned to stay away from the man. We heard a couple of neighbors say that they felt like he got what he deserved.

One of the strangest things about this incident was that in the apartment when the patrol officer arrived, there was a German Shepherd dog. The officer put a leash on the dog and put him in a closet. When we checked on the dog, he appeared to be very calm. We did find out from the second-floor neighbor that the deceased was frequently seen in the neighborhood walking the dog.

We went back in the apartment and checked the deceased out a little closer. I'm not a doctor, but the separation of the penis and testes appeared to be very precise, as if someone had cut them off. My partner, the patrol officer, and myself were having a discussion on what we thought might have happened. After receiving the information that the deceased was a sex offender and finding out that the neighbors did not like the guy, we were thinking, *did a neighbor get into the apartment and cut off the guys penis and testicles?*

Before the medical examiner arrived, we were noticing that much of the food in the kitchen, like boxes of cereal were all on the floor. A few of the cabinets were open and the contents just spilled all over the counter. The trash container was turned over and the contents strewn around the kitchen. We also noticed what appeared to be dog feces throughout the entire apartment. Not knowing if this was a real crime scene, we had to step gingerly while in the apartment.

The medical examiner arrived and started an examination of the body. The doctor said that he had never seen anything like this before. As only doctors would do, he got down on the floor and with gloves on. He examined the area where there used to be a penis and testicles. After a few minutes, he stood and took a deep breath. "I think there are teeth marks in the cavity where the penis and testes used to be."
Well, when he said that, I was thinking...*what kind of kinky sex was this guy involved in?*

The doctor got down on the floor again and continued to examine the area of the missing parts. After a few minutes, he stood and repeated that there were definitely teeth marks inside the open cavity. He asked Frank and I if we wanted to take a look...we declined. We stood around talking about different scenarios on how and why something like this could have happened. Naturally, Frank and I, being cops were thinking that a neighbor who didn't like a sex offender living in their neighborhood, broke in and performed some nasty surgery on our victim.

While we were waiting for the morgue wagon to arrive, the dog started to bark. We had actually forgot that he was in the closet. Frank opened the door and we let the dog out. Frank hooked the leash to a table so the dog could not run around. The dog was very calm and just laid on the kitchen floor.

The body was removed from the house and taken to the Medical Examiners Officer where an autopsy would be conducted. We discussed the incident with the doctor when we were outside the apartment. The doctor said that he feels with certainty that the man had probably experienced some type of medical event and died on the floor. The doctor said that why the man was naked would probably never be known. He went on to say that because there was no break into the apartment, he feels that when the man fell on the floor, he was probably there for a long period of time. He further stated the dog, after scrounging around for food in the cabinets, decided that the penis and testicles were there for the taking. The doctor said that the teeth marks on the cavity were large and could definitely be the dog's. He said he hopes that the autopsy will give him a better understanding of how the man died. The autopsy would also allow him to dissect the cavity closer to measure the teeth marks. He said if his theory is correct, he would rule the death a natural death. He felt that the removal of the penis and testes by the dog was done after the man had died.

When we were leaving the apartment, we were approached by an elderly man who lived on the second floor. He was inquiring about what happened. He also asked about the dog. We probably should not have told him everything, but we did. We told him our theory about what the dog did to the deceased. He paused for a few seconds and said, "What will happen to the dog?" I told him that we had notified the city dog pound and they would be picking up the dog. He started to walk away, stopped, and said, "Can I take the dog?"

Frank and I looked at each other and were amazed that this elderly man would want to take the dog after what we had told him. The man was serious. "I think I can make a nice home for that dog."
I asked the man to step out on the sidewalk for a minute. I told him that asking about the dog was a nice gesture. I also said, "Sir, we have conveyed to you what that dog did to his master. If you want that dog we could probably arrange it. You need to remember this...one night when you're sitting in your favorite chair in your underwear watching the late show, and the dog remembers the nice meal he got from his old master he might just chomp down on your privates. German Shepherds have great memories and very strong jaws. Do you still think you want that dog?"

The elderly man seemed to be gasping for breath after what I told him. He turned and as he walked away, he said, "Detective, you're right...fuck that dog."

A week later we met with the doctor who did the autopsy. He said that his examination revealed that the cause of death was a diabetic coma. The man most likely became unconscious and fell to the kitchen floor. He also had some trauma to his head from the fall. The doctor stated that the man may have been alive for a while, but without medical assistance he died. He said that upon examination of the area of the missing penis and testes, he feels without a doubt that the dog ate that area. He said that for a big hungry dog, that area would be considered...*low hanging fruit.*

Conversation # 23

Here's a short story about what goes on when I have breakfast with my retired cop friends.

As we sit in the diner having breakfast, the war stories start. Just a bunch of old retired homicide cops that love to get together and talk about our time on the police department. The breakfast meeting is something that we all look forward to, even though we have heard most of the stories over and over through the years.

Several of the retired cops now have hearing problems, so the stories get quite loud. Sometimes the waitress will ask us to tone it down a little, but we don't. The more coffee we drink, the louder we get. It seems like everyone wants to talk at the same time.
"Hold it down boys," says Thelma. She's our waitress and has been saying that to us for quite a few years. We acknowledge her but ignore her. She doesn't care if we hold it down or not. She fills our cups and moves around the restaurant with the quickness of a cat.

The ages of our retired cop crew ranges from the '60s to the late '80s. We have guys that worked in the police department going back as far as the 1950s. I would estimate that the guys have over three hundred combined years of law enforcement service.

I look forward to the breakfast get-togethers. On my way there, I'm usually thinking of some of the stories I want to talk about. We now have some guys who will start a story but can't finish it. When we see someone struggling to come up with the finish or try to remember a name from the past, we jump in. Sometimes it goes like this...*hey, you remember that guy, the big guy, you know who I'm talking about, the tall guy with the red hair.*

The rest of the retirees work real hard to try and help. It might take a few minutes, but eventually someone will blurt out the name of the big tall guy with red hair. When someone is struggling to finish a story, we feel that it's our obligation to help. We helped each other for many years in the police department, so there is no reason to stop now.

I'm sure that the other customers in the diner get a real police education from our loud talking. We have actually had people come over to our table and thank us for our service.

"Please boys, you need to hold it down." Thelma speaks, but she's moving so fast, most don't even hear her as she hustles by holding more trays of food than you would think a woman her age could carry.

Pete hollers to her, "You're the prettiest waitress in the place."

She delivers her trays and walks by, giving Pete a kiss on the cheek. She then calls him the biggest liar in the world.

Joe shouts across the table, "Do you guys remember the riots in sixty-eight when we worked twelve hours on and twelve hours off?"

There are eight of us at the table, only two can hear Joe. Frustrated, Joe gets loud and repeats his question. Now he has a majority, so he continues.

"I didn't go home for three days. I slept in the basement of the old Central District."

"So, what's your point?" hollers Augie from the other end of the table.

Joe jumps up and gets louder. "My point is that we didn't get paid for all those hours we worked. Hell, today if they work one hour past their shift, they get paid big bucks. We stopped that riot in sixty-eight. I'm not sure how we did it, but we did."

Eddie, who has been silent as he takes it all in, speaks up. "Do you guys think we will get a raise in our pension this year?"

Before Eddie can continue, several guys start talking at the same time. Don, who is the unofficial expert on pensions and anything to do with money, speaks up.

"Listen guys, we have talked about this in the past. You will not be getting any more than we usually get each year. The city is strapped for money. So, dig into your savings and spend it; you won't take it with you when you're called to your final roll call."

134

Silence sets in for a few seconds as if the news of not getting any money in our pensions is paramount to a death sentence.
Pete hollers to Augie, "If I had your money, I wouldn't worry about anything."
Augie laughs but does not respond.
A few minutes later Augie shouts across the table at Pete, "I worked my butt off after I retired, so that I could enjoy the back nine of my life."

Thelma sees that we have finished our breakfast. "Can I get you boys more coffee or are you flying high on caffeine? Joe, you forgot to tell the story about when the cop fell asleep in his police car with the door open. The car slipped out of gear and went backwards hitting a tree, taking the door off. I love when you tell that story."
Joe just laughs and knows that we have all heard that story too many times; we just can't remember who the cop was in the car. Could it have been the tall, red-headed guy?

The table gets quiet, we can't think of any more stories or the caffeine has fractured our brains. We do our usual ritual of splitting the bill. It doesn't matter what you had; we just add in a big tip for Thelma and split it. Don is the collector of the money. Thelma always gets a big tip. I have even seen guys give her something extra as they leave the diner.

When outside, no matter what the weather is, there is always time for one more story. I look forward to those get-togethers, you just don't know how many of them you have left.

If the story comes up again, I'll remember that tall, red-headed guy's name.... maybe.

Conversation # 24

Well, hang with me a little longer; we're getting close to the end. I've enjoyed our conversations up to this point...how about you?

I have enjoyed sharing my stories with you. However, there comes a time when you need to just move on. I do have some more stories, but I'll keep them to myself. Some are crazier than what I have already told you...so, the thought of federal prison does not appeal to me...*just kidding.*

Over the past several years while writing my books, I have encouraged other police officers to write their book. I know there are many of my colleagues that have great stories. I hear the same answer from them all the time...*I just can't put it together, I'm not an author.* I tell them that I'm not really an author either. I'm just a guy who likes to tell stories. I also have enjoyed writing a couple crime novels and a children's book.

The children's book came about because I have eight grandchildren. When they were younger, they always enjoyed me telling them stories. I would tell them stories about when I was a youngster. They didn't know it at the time, but I made up all the stories. When the older grandchildren found out I was writing books, they asked if I would write a children's book.

The children's book is titled, *The Secret Zoo*. The book is about a bunch of kids that live near a zoo. The kids know that the zoo keeper, Captain Corky, can talk to the animals. The story revolves around the kids in the book planning on going in the zoo and also trying to talk to the animals.

I hope that one day, my grandchildren will be reading the book to their children. I might not be here, but I would be really proud to know that they will tell their children that their great-grandfather wrote the book.

The novels that I have written have amazed me. It's fascinating what goes through your mind when you begin the process of writing a novel. I'm often asked where I came up with the plot and the characters. My answer is very simple; you have to have some basic knowledge of the subject matter.

I was in law enforcement for over twenty-five years, so therefore I know how to write about crime. I've worked in some units within the police department that have given me plenty of material for my books.

I was a cop, so I write about police work. If you're a doctor, you write about medical stuff. If you're a teacher, you write about teaching. Writing a novel is really that simple. If you're a gastroenterologist, you write about people making an ass of themselves.

As we have already talked about, I worked in patrol when I first went on the Baltimore City Police Department. I had the unbelievable opportunity to walk a foot post in the neighborhood I grew up in. That alone is something that very few police officers have the opportunity to do.

I moved away from the neighborhood I grew up in when I was seventeen to go in the Marines. I returned to the neighborhood when I was twenty-one as a police officer. Some would think that it would be very difficult to police the neighborhood that you grew up in. I have written about it and yes, it had its challenges. I look back on it and would not change those times for anything.

Back in the mid '60s, most police officers walked foot patrol in the Baltimore City neighborhoods. It was as if you were the sheriff of a small town, a very small town. The eight hours you walked in the neighborhood, you were the enforcer of the peace. Even at the ripe age of twenty-one, you were supposed to come up with the all the answers.

I can remember going into homes where people twice my age were arguing or sometimes fighting. I always wondered what they thought of a very young police officer coming in and telling them why they should calm down. What training gives you that ability at such a young age? Where do you get the words to convince people to stop arguing or fighting? Do they have a respect or a fear of the uniform? Does the badge and gun demand respect?

I wasn't married at the time I started on the police department. Where did I draw from to come up with the words that would solve family problems? I didn't have any senior officers with me when I went into the homes. I'm not sure how I did it, but somehow, I did it.

137

There were times when you needed to take action and make an arrest. I always wanted things to turn out without that happening.

The neighborhood I worked in was very blue collar. The men worked hard all week to support their families. On the weekend they liked to party a little. When I did have to make an arrest for a domestic disturbance, I would always go back to that house in a few days and talk to the couple. I've had times when I arrested someone and we actually became good friends. It was important as a young rookie to make as many friends as possible. You never knew when you would need their help.

After working in patrol and walking that foot post for a few years, I got assigned to the Vice Unit. I have talked a lot about those days working vice in this book and in my first book.

I later worked in the Robbery Unit. I was detailed with the Baltimore office of the FBI to work on bank robberies. Working with the FBI gave me a bigger picture of law enforcement. I have written in my books that in the early '70s in Baltimore, it was like the wild west. Banks were being robbed at a record pace. There were days when several banks would be robbed. We even had a bank that was robbed three times in one week. Some of the culprits were professional; most were guys just in need of some quick money.

We were so busy, it seemed like we went from one bank robbery to the next. I worked with some fine FBI agents. Being an agency that big and having so many resources, proved to be very beneficial to our success.

I was always amazed at the bank robbers we caught; they knew how to work the system. They were aware that if they confessed to city cops they were facing thirty years in a Maryland prison. If they confessed to the FBI agents they would get twenty-five years in a federal prison. The federal prisons had the reputation of being much more lenient than Maryland prisons. I was told that there was a federal prison in Pennsylvania that actually had a three-hole golf course.

I mentioned earlier that there were some stories I could not tell in fear of going to federal prison. Well, if I had to go, I'm in for the one with the golf course.

It really didn't matter to us city guys who bank robbers confessed to...as long as they were caught and off the streets of Baltimore.

After a few years in the Robbery Unit, I moved over to the Homicide Unit. I talked previously in this book about working in the Homicide Unit. After all these years in retirement, I still think about the murders that I didn't solve, or my squad didn't solve.

I think the one homicide that bugs me the most is the murder of Doctor Sebastian Russo in 1981. Dr. Russo was a family doctor who charged five bucks for a visit. If you brought your family, it might be ten bucks. He lived on one side of the street and his medical office was on the other side.

I knew the neighborhood where the doctor practiced. My dad was a patient of Dr. Russo's. In the evening around 7 P.M., the line would stretch down two city blocks with people waiting to see the doctor.

On the night he was murdered, a black male walked into the doctor's office. He walked past several people waiting to see Dr. Russo. He obviously knew the layout of the office. He walked straight back to where the doctor saw patients. He shot the doctor and walked out past the people still in the waiting area. No one said they heard the shots. No one could describe the shooter, other than being a tall black male. I won't go into the entire investigation, but I will say that the investigators on the scene that night did not do a good job.

I received the assignment the day after the shooting. I had three detectives assigned to work with me. The murder of Dr. Russo was never solved. It is still in the cold case files in the Baltimore City Police Department.

After the doctor's murder, the neighborhood residents and the local business owners erected a large clock at the intersection close to where Dr. Russo lived.

After thirty-six years of the clock being at that intersection, it was knocked down in a traffic accident in 2016. In 2017, after contributions were obtained from the residents and business owners in the area, a new clock was erected on the same corner.

I heard about the dedication and unveiling of the new clock. I attended the ceremony. I was there standing in the crowd. I did not tell anyone that I was the supervisor of the murder investigation of Dr. Russo.

While in the crowd, I heard people talking about the investigation and how they perceived the doctor was murdered. I then felt compelled to speak up and try to put to rest some of the rumors about the murder. After a short period of time, I had a small crowd listening to my account of what happened. We were then invited to a nearby restaurant for coffee and pastries.

I stayed in the restaurant for a couple hours talking to different people about the murder. When the doctor was murdered, his daughter was fifteen years old. I had the pleasure of meeting her at this dedication and she was now fifty-one years old. While talking to her, I could not help but to think how she must have felt thirty-six years ago as a teenager, finding out that her dad was murdered. I felt compelled to tell her everything I knew about the investigation, up to the point when I retired. I told her that the investigation is continuing in the cold case unit of the police department. I told her that unless someone comes forward with information, the case may never be solved.

The doctor's daughter had moved away from that neighborhood. She had only returned for the dedication. She told me she could not find the courage over the years to come back to that neighborhood. I was glad I had the opportunity to talk to her about her father. Before I left the restaurant, I went to my car and got my first book, *Cop Stories-The Few, The Proud, The Ugly*. I signed it and gave it to her. The book has a whole chapter on the investigation of her father's murder.

I left there with the satisfaction of knowing that I may have brought some closure to her about her father's murder. I assured her that the cold case unit would always be open to any leads that came in on Dr. Russo's murder.

I hope that someday in her lifetime, she gets the final closure that she has been waiting for all these many years, with the arrest of the killer.

Conversation # 25

As I approach the end of our conversations, I, like everyone else, have been thinking about the mass shootings around the country, especially the one in Parkland, Florida.

The Parkland shooting occurred on Valentine's Day, February 14, 2018. The mass shooting was inside the Marjory Stoneman Douglas High School. Seventeen students and faculty were gunned down by a crazed, confused, nineteen-year-old, who was a former student at the school.

The shooter, who I refuse to use his name in my book, entered the school with an AR-15 assault rifle. He began his carnage which lasted only six minutes. He then left the school, mixed in with the students who were running for their lives, and casually went to a Walmart to purchase a soda. He was later spotted walking in a neighborhood close to the school. He was apprehended by the police without incident.

I'm sure you have read many accounts of what happened or what didn't happen at that school. There has been plenty of blame put on law enforcement for not following up on many leads that may have prevented this shooting. I'm not going to criticize what went wrong in this book. I do however, have a close connection with someone who led the investigation of that horrible shooting. I will get to him shortly.

In the United States, we have more mass shootings than any other country in the world. The FBI designates a mass shooting as an incident where there are at least four victims. I'm not going to attempt to list the mass shootings that have occurred over the past several years. I'm sure through all the news coverage of these events you are aware of when and how they happened.

I am also not going to get into my thoughts on gun control, other than to say, I would ban the AR-15. I would also ban the assault rifles that have been used in these mass murders. I believe in the 2nd Amendment. I also believe that anyone purchasing a gun should have mandatory training in the use of that gun. They should go through an extensive background check and be issued a license that would need to be renewed every three years. The renewal would include additional training and another background investigation. I would also like to see a federal agency established that would track gun purchases in the United States.

I know the ATF does a great job tracking guns, but it's after the fact. If we are serious in this country, let's stop talking about it and get it done.

I know that many people are stuck on the debate about selling guns to people with a mental condition. How do you determine who has a mental problem? Unless it is documented in medical records, there would be no way a gun salesman would know. The salesman would need to have access to those records; this is where a federal agency would come into play.

At the current time, medical records are protected by privacy laws. Just the term mental is used in so many ways these days. We see a person acting strange, we say they're mental, we get in an argument with someone, we say they're mental, we sometimes hear things about our friends and neighbors and we say they're mental. Hell, I have been called mental. I'm sure some of you have been called mental. I think the word mental is thrown around like: stupid, ugly, crazy, and some others.

The real reason I'm writing about the shooting in Parkland, Florida is because I have somewhat of a personal stake in the investigation. The high school where the shootings occurred is located in Broward County, Florida. My son, David, is a detective sergeant in the Homicide Unit with the Broward County Sheriff's Agency. He supervised the investigation of this mass school shooting. I have talked to him about this tragic incident on several occasions. Most of what we have talked about is routine stuff from a retired homicide supervisor to a present-day homicide supervisor...just a father/son conversation.

As I have told you in prior conversations in this book, I was a detective sergeant in the Homicide Unit in the Baltimore City Police Department. Dave and I talk frequently about murder investigations. I hope that doesn't sound too morbid. Because we both spent time working on murders, who better to talk to than your father about a murder.

I know that there are more forensic investigative tools available today than when I was investigating murders. Even though they have more tools to work with, I can assure you that the basic principles of investigating a homicide will never change. The investigation involves a knowledge of forensic pathology, a thorough crime scene investigation, collection and preservation of evidence, locating witnesses, interviewing techniques, compiling the case for court, and expert testimony in court.

When I talk to my son on the phone, I know he feels comfortable talking to me about the murder investigations he is working on. He understands that I have been there and done that.

In a city as dangerous as Baltimore, which has been on the list of the top ten most dangerous cities in the nation for as long as I can remember, he knows first-hand that I have handled more than my share of murders. He also knows about Baltimore because he was on the Baltimore City PD for six years before he resigned and went to Florida. I actually enjoy having these conversations with him. We do discuss other things besides murder.

When you talk about these mass shootings, you hear all kinds of solutions. Most are well intended, but you really need to weigh what you're hearing against the actual facts. I'm not knocking anyone who wants to discuss a solution. I'm only saying that I would really hope that anyone suggesting a solution give it some thought.

For instance, to say all guns need to be taken off the streets of America is ridiculous. I'm not sure how that would be done. Would there be an agency that would come to your home looking for guns? Would there be new laws that would allow police to just stop you and search for a gun? We know that history tells us about a real evil man that wanted to take all the guns from the people...his name was Adolph Hitler.

I think that most of us would agree that we now live in a very violent nation. To begin to solve the problem, we need to start somewhere. I think that banning the sale of weapons that are made for the sole purpose to kill people is a good start. If it cost money to establish an agency that oversees and investigates the banning of assault weapons, conducting thorough background investigations, providing training, and having a state of the art tracking system...I think the majority of Americans would not object to some kind of tax to pay for it.

While I'm talking about my son, let me jump in and reiterate how the Ellwood family has made its mark in law enforcement over the years. My son, Dave, is the fourth generation of our family to serve in law enforcement. My grandfather, John Dunn, served in the Baltimore Police Department in the late 1800's. He was my mother's father, her maiden name being Dunn. We have photos of him in full uniform riding a bicycle in a park in Baltimore. I have a small book that he carried in which he kept records of his arrest. We have also donated several photos of him to the police museum in the Baltimore City Police headquarters building.

Next in the generation flow would be my father, Dick Ellwood senior. He started in the Baltimore City Police Department in 1939. He was thirty-four years old when he joined the department. At his age at the time, it was considered coming on the police department late in life. Most police officers join police work in their early twenty's.

My dad was the most typical police officer you could ever imagine. If you wanted to paint a picture of what a cop should act like or even look like, he's your man. He was a patrolman his entire time on the police department. Not that he could not have made rank, it was just that he was happy in the job he had. He was a traffic cop for most of the time on the police department. He never drove a car. He walked to work from our home in the inner city on many occasions. If he didn't walk, he would ride the trolley. I have talked about him in my prior book, *Cop Stories-The Few, The Proud, The Ugly.*

My dad was always ready, willing, and able to help anyone in our neighborhood. It did not seem like an evening would go by that he would not have someone come to the house with a problem. I can remember on summer nights, people would come over. They would sit on the front marble steps and go over their problem with him. It could be a traffic ticket, family problems, parental problems, or anything that someone would think he could help them with. He also helped some men from the neighborhood get on the police department. He was very friendly with the police physician and the bosses in the police department. He used that influence to get these guys on the department.

When I went on the Baltimore City Police Department, that made me the third generation. When I started walking the streets of Baltimore, every cop that I came in contact with knew my dad. I would go in places and when they saw the name tag on my uniform coat, they would ask if I was Dick Ellwood's son. It made me extremely proud that so many people had such nice things to say about him. It was also nice that I got a lot of free meals by just being his son.

I started on the police department in 1964. I was actually sworn in on New Year's Eve, December 31, 1964. I officially started on the department in 1965. I won't bore you with stuff I have already told you in our prior conversations.

I will say that it was exciting to follow in my father and grandfather's footsteps. And believe me, they were big footsteps to follow.

I had a great career in law enforcement. I retired after twenty-five years on the job. I could have stayed longer, but I was eligible to retire and was offered a very lucrative job with a major insurance company.

I now enjoy some quality time together with my fellow retired police officers. We get together for breakfast, retirement meetings, card games, and yes, sadly, at too many funerals. Even though policing has changed a lot over the years, we retirees can still relate to what police officers are going through today.

During my time on the police department, we didn't see all the anger toward law enforcement like we see today. It seems that some people today would not be happy even if they had a police officer stationed on their front porch.

You really need a thick skin in today's world of policing. You're expected to make decisions in seconds and then months later, a judge or jury will decide if that split-second decision was legal or did it offend and violate someone's rights.

I saw this short definition of police work somewhere and don't know who wrote it. I'm going to share it with you.

To fight when others fold, pursue while others retreat, conquer while others quit, and make right when all is wrong.

I'm also going to share a poem with you that has a lot of meaning on what a police officer is made of. I don't know who wrote this either, but I'm sure they won't mine me sharing their fine work.

When the Lord was creating cops, he was into his sixth day of overtime when an angel appeared and said, "You're doing a lot of fiddling around on this one."

And the Lord said, "Have you read the specs on this order, a police officer has to be able to run five miles through alleys in the dark, scale walls, enter homes the health inspector wouldn't touch, and not wrinkle his uniform."

"He has to be able to sit in an undercover car all day on a stakeout, cover a homicide scene that night, canvass the neighborhood for witnesses, and testify in court the next day."

"He has to be in top physical condition at all times, running on black coffee and half-eaten meals.
And he has to have six pairs of hands."
The angel shook her head slowly and said, "Six pairs of hands... no way."

"It's not the hands that are causing me problems," said the Lord, "it's the three pair of eyes an officer has to have."

"That's on the standard model?" asked the angel.

The Lord nodded. "One pair that sees through a bulge in a pocket before he asks, can I see what's in there, sir?" When he already knows and wishes he'd taken that accounting job. He has another pair here on the side of his head for his partner's safety. And another pair of eyes here in front that can look reassuringly at a bleeding victim and say, you'll be all right ma'am, when he knows it isn't so."

"Lord," said the angel, touching his sleeve, "rest and work on this tomorrow."

"I can't," said the Lord, "I already have a model that can talk a 250-pound drunk

into a patrol car without incident and feed a family of five on a civil service paycheck."

The angel circled the model of the police officer very slowly, "Can it think?" she asked.

"You bet," said the Lord. "It can tell you the elements of a hundred crimes; recite Miranda warnings in its sleep; detain, investigate, search, and arrest a gang member on the street in less time than it takes five learned judges to debate the legality of the stop ... and still it keeps its sense of humor. This officer also has phenomenal personal control. He can deal with crime scenes painted in hell, coax a confession from a child abuser, comfort a murder victim's family, and then read in the daily paper how law enforcement isn't sensitive to the rights of criminal suspects."

Finally, the angel bent over and ran her finger across the cheek of the peace officer. "There's a leak," she pronounced. "I told you that you were trying to put too much into this model."

"That's not a leak" said the lord. "It's a tear."

"What's the tear for?" asked the angel.

"It's for bottled-up emotions, for fallen comrades, for commitment to that funny piece of cloth called the American flag, and for justice."

"You're a genius," said the angel.

The Lord looked somber and said, "I didn't put it there."

Now, back to me finishing up on this book and our continued conversations.

I just want to end with saying that our law enforcement people these days have a very tough job. It doesn't seem like there's a day that goes by that you don't read about how they want to change policing in this country. I would imagine that most people who will read this book grew up with respect for our police officers. If you have had a bad encounter with a police officer; you need to ask yourself...what caused the bad encounter? Was it my fault?

I may be older than some of my readers. I had a lot of respect for the officers that walked the beat in my neighborhood when I was growing up. I know my dad was a cop and that sure had a lot to do with how I felt. I remember the cops in our neighborhood with much respect, admiration, and appreciation.

Back then, we didn't have all the crime that goes on today. We might have gotten caught drinking beer on a Saturday night, throwing eggs at vehicles, being too loud late at night, or robbing banks.... I'm kidding about robbing banks, just wanted to keep your attention.

I'm sure that after reading my book, you will come to the conclusion that I had a great time in my twenty-five years on the police department. I know there were some dicey times where I could have gotten into some trouble. I want you to know that the serious times on the job definitely outweighed some of the foolish things I have talked about in this book. Who wants to read about all the good things a cop does? I can assure you that there isn't a day that goes by in a cop's shift that he doesn't do several very good deeds.

I can honestly say that I did my absolute best wherever I was assigned. I also made it a point to have fun. In police work, you need to have fun. It's a serious job, but without a little fun, it could be boring.

Maybe, you're thinking that cops in my stories may have overdone the fun part sometime, but what the hell...nobody got hurt. So, what if I almost lost some police cars, so what if I left a guy in a graveyard overnight, so what if we ran over a robbery suspect, so what if I robbed my passengers in a cab, so what if we sent a guy to the federal building to register a machine gun, so what if we had a whiskey drinking contest...who cares, nobody got hurt. I did a lot of good things, but who wants to read about good things...so we will move on.

However, if you want to hear about some really good things that I was honored to do, thanks to the police department having faith in my performance. I was the first detective to the attend the homicide school at the FBI Academy in Quantico, Virginia. I was the first member of the department to attend the National Fire Academy in Emmitsburg, Maryland. I was the first from the department to attend the Federal Law Enforcement Training Center in Glencoe, Georgia. I attended the Francis Glessner Lee Death Investigation school conducted by Dr. Russell Fisher, the pioneer of forensic pathology in death investigations. I attended the BNDD (Bureau of Narcotics & Dangerous Drugs) school in Washington, D.C. which is now known as the DEA (Drug Enforcement Agency). I attended the University of Maryland Fire Rescue Institute. I lectured at the University of Baltimore. I taught a fire investigation course at the Community College of Baltimore. In the mid '70s I assisted with training Maryland State Troopers in homicide investigation. I taught arson investigation in the Baltimore Police Academy.

Now, do you like me a little better?

Let me end by telling you something about cops. If you're around cops at work or with them at social functions, you will see them joking, mostly with other cops. It's something that we have in common...you can call it *the thin blue line* or anything you want to call it. It's a mechanism that allows a police officer to talk about their job with their peers, people who understand what they're going through. A cop knows he can to come to work every day knowing that no matter what happens, his guys in blue are there for him or her.

I didn't include in the writing of this book about many other situations that I've been involved in... like being shot at, being stabbed, being beat up, or being thrown through a window. I wanted to give you my best overall picture of police work. Who wants to hear about cops getting hurt? I do consider myself extremely fortunate. My injuries while a cop were all minor compared to some cops that were seriously injured or those that made the ultimate sacrifice.

For those of you that are cops, you will find this next section very true. For those of you who are not, this will give you a little insight as to why the men and women in blue are the way we are. Again, I'm not sure who wrote this or even where I got it, but I like it.

Once the badge goes on, it never comes off, whether they can see it or not. It fuses to the soul through adversity, fear, and adrenaline, and no one who has ever worn it with pride, integrity, and guts, can stand by and let it be abused.

When a good cop leaves the job and retires to a better life, many are jealous. Some are pleased and yet others, who may have already retired, wonder. We wonder if he knows what he is leaving behind, because we already know. We know, for example, that after a lifetime of camaraderie that few experience, it will remain as a longing for those past times. We know in the law enforcement life there is a fellowship which lasts long after the uniforms are hung up in the back of the closet.

We know even if he throws them away, they will be on him with every step and breath that remains in his life. We also know how the very bearing of the man speaks of what he was and, in his heart, still is.

These are the burdens of the job. You will still look at people suspiciously, still see what others do not see or choose to ignore and always will look at the rest of the law enforcement world with a respect for what they do; only grown in a lifetime of knowing. Never think for one moment you are escaping from that life. You are only escaping the job and merely being allowed to leave active duty.

So what I wish for those that leave is that whenever you ease into retirement, in your heart you never forget for one moment that you are still a member of the greatest fraternity the world has ever known.

As I am winding down, I just want to say that I'm not sure if there are any more books in the future for me to write. I'm getting old, and actually I think I'm running out of stories. It has been an absolute pleasure over the years to know that people read my books. There is no greater feeling to a writer than to have someone tell them how much they enjoyed their book. As I have mentioned earlier, I have always wanted to write as if I were just having a conversation with you. I think we've had some really good conversations in this book.

During my years of selling books, I have talked with many young men and women who are considering getting into law enforcement. I have always told them that being a cop is more than a job. You have to have mental and physical skills to survive. It may be the most demanding job of any profession. When you take that oath, you become a vital part of society.

I can understand why a young person might want to be a cop. The salary is a lot more tempting than when I joined. I've seen statistics that show that the median income for a police officer in the United States is $61,600. I know that locally in the Baltimore area the starting salary is about $45,000. Just to give you an idea of what my starting salary was many years ago...let's just say it was $40,000 less than the current Baltimore area starting salary.

There are however, lots of perks in law enforcement jobs. Many police departments today have twenty-year retirements. You don't have to work at a desk or cubicle. You join a bond that you will not find in any other profession. No day's work is the same for a police officer. You will join a group of people with a great sense of humor and have the ability to make light of the dangerous work they do. For the most part in today's society, you will come across the majority of people that recognize the sacrifice and dedication police officers put forth on a daily basis.

As I attempt to end our conversations, I'll leave you with these final thoughts.

Being a police officer was one of the greatest accomplishments of my life. I know that I followed in some awesome footsteps. My dad would have been very proud of my career in law enforcement. Now, my son takes up the torch and who knows, maybe there will be another Ellwood in law enforcement someday.

The only other accomplishment in my life that compares with police work, was being a United States Marine. I gave the Marine Corps four years of my young life. At first, I thought I had made a big mistake by joining the Marines. As time went on, I was hooked on the tradition, the comradery, the Esprit de corps, the enthusiasm, the devotion, and most of all, the common spirit existing in the members of a very elite group.

Like Marines, you could say that police officers are "Gung Ho" ...which many have described as extremely overzealous or enthusiastic. I guess because I have served in both, I can say with much certainty that it is true.

As I recap some of our conversations...I can't believe I put four years in the Marines. I served with Charles Whitman, the Texas tower shooter. I locked up Mickey Mantle. I wrote five books since retiring. I've had twenty surgeries that are mostly tennis related. I shot a dog the first day on the job. I locked up thirteen prostitutes in one night. I got thrown through a window by a pimp. I'm a high school dropout who finished college. I taught criminal justice in college. I handled a murder on death row. I can't stand the sight of blood but worked in the homicide unit for eleven years. I joined the Marines to travel and was stationed forty miles from home. I got measured for a jock strap by the pastor of my church. I'm exhausted...I better stop here.

Well, all good conversations must come to an end. I have enjoyed sharing my stories and thoughts with you.

If there is another book in me, I will see you down the road...if not, "Semper Fi".

COP STORIES II

COP STORIES II

COP STORIES II